SOCIAL WOR

A GUIDE TO
THE CHILDREN ACT 1975

AUSTRALIA
The Law Book Company Ltd.
Sydney : Melbourne : Brisbane

CANADA AND U.S.A.
The Carswell Company Ltd.
Agincourt, Ontario

INDIA
N.M. Tripathi Private Ltd.
Bombay

ISRAEL
Steimatzky's Agency Ltd.
Jerusalem: Tel Aviv: Haifa

MALAYSIA : SINGAPORE : BRUNEL
Malayan Law Journal (Pte.) Ltd.
Singapore

NEW ZEALAND
Sweet and Maxwell (N.Z.) Ltd.
Wellington

PAKISTAN
Pakistan Law House
Karachi

SOCIAL WORK AND LAW

A GUIDE
TO
THE CHILDREN ACT 1975

by

JENNIFER TERRY, M.SC., LL.B., DIP.SOC.AD.

Barrister of the Inner Temple; Social Worker

LONDON
SWEET & MAXWELL
1976

Published in 1976 by
Sweet & Maxwell Ltd. of
11 New Fetter Lane, London.
Photoset by Red Lion Setters, London.
Printed in Great Britain by
Fletcher & Son Ltd., Norwich

ISBN 0 421 21690 5 ✓

010 7099

©
Jennifer Terry
1976

PREFACE

The aim of this book is to present the Children Act 1975 and its implications in a form which is readily understandable to social workers and others involved in the social services. The growing complexity of the law relating to children is self evident and in the absence of consolidating legislation the non-lawyer has the task of weaving his way through the relevant statutes in order to comprehend the law on this subject. For this reason an explanatory guide to the new Act seems to be necessary at this stage.

The 1975 Act constantly refers to and amends previous legislation and understanding its provisions is difficult without a close working knowledge of all the previous Acts relating to children. This is particularly evident in Part II of the Act where there is an intermeshing of the provisions relating to custodianship with the provisions of the Guardianship of Minors Acts 1971 and 1973. Substantial amendments are made to the Adoption Act 1958, the Children Act 1948 and the Children and Young Persons Act 1969. The Scottish law is also amended by the Act. This book examines the implications of these amendments and sets them within the context of the existing legislation. The book provides the social worker, the social administrator and the social work student with a detailed outline of the Act and discusses how it will affect their practice. It does not however deal with the more intricate points of law and the social worker should seek professional legal advice should such problems arise. The dearth of text books on law for social workers has been highlighted by the report of the Study Group set up by the Central Council for Education and Training in Social Work entitled *Legal Studies in Social Work Education*, and this is beginning to be remedied. Certainly it is now becoming accepted that social workers can only employ their skills effectively and sensitively if they work from a basis of knowledge which includes an understanding of their legal powers and obligations.

As this book is intended to serve as a convenient reference work on the effects of the Act, a Table of Statutes and a detailed Index is included. The book should be read in conjunction with a copy of the Act for, although many people find Acts of Parliament difficult to read with understanding at first, this does improve with practice. The Act will only be implemented gradually over the next two or three years to ensure that the necessary resources are available to carry out its provisions. To enable a consistency of style however the book is written as though all the provisions of the Act have come into force. Those provisions which are not in force by the date of publication have been asterisked to show that they have yet to be implemented. They will be brought into force gradually by statutory instrument. All the sections of the Act which are in force are not asterisked.

January 1976   JENNIFER A. TERRY

CONTENTS

TABLE OF STATUTES

[All references are to paragraph numbers]

1 The Scope of the Act

The Children Act 1975 (which is referred to in this book as the Act or 1975 Act) is the most important piece of legislation in the child care field since the Children and Young Persons Act 1969. The framework and scope of the Act is outlined in this chapter and the provisions of the Act are examined in more detail in subsequent chapters. Since 1969 a complex interaction of factors has made the climate ripe for further reforms in the law relating to children. These ensured that Dr. David Owen's private Member's Bill introduced in 1974 received much attention and support and was later substantially followed in the Government Bill which resulted in this Act.

1. The first of these factors leading up to reform was the Report of the Departmental Committee on the Adoption of Children (Cmnd. 5107) (which is referred to throughout as the Houghton Committee) published in 1972. The Committee was set up in 1969 to consider the "law, policy and procedure on the adoption of children and what changes are desirable." It conducted a great deal of research into adoption and its recommendations were well received, but until 1974 there had been no attempt to translate these into legislation.

2. The study by Jane Rowe and Lydia Lambert, *Children who Wait*, was another important factor in this respect. Their study showed that about 2,000 children linger in long term care because their parents refuse to consent to adoption. A further 5,000 children in long term care were thought to need something short of adoption, such as a secure fostering situation for which the law did not provide. The harmful effects on some children of residential care are well documented and studies have shown again and again that for the majority of children in long term care a good fostering placement or adoption, where that is appropriate, are preferable to care in a residential establishment. The high cost of residential care in an

establishment such as a children's home has also been used as an argument (perhaps not the most valid one) against this form of substitute care.

3. The impact of the Maria Colwell case and the consequent Committee of Inquiry Report is another factor which has created an impetus for reform. The reality of child abuse, which workers in the social service and medical fields had long been aware of, was brought dramatically to public attention by the media's focus on the tragedy of Maria Colwell and amongst the clamour to apportion blame there emerged a genuine feeling of wanting to avoid such tragedies in the future. So-called "tug of love" cases, that is, disputes between foster parents and natural parents as to who is going to have the care of the child, have also been the subject of public concern and have indicated further areas where it was felt the law was inadequate and where the interests of the child were not properly safeguarded.

The changes brought in by the Act fall into three main areas: changes in the law relating to adoption; the introduction of a new status midway between that of foster parent and adopter called "custodianship"; and last, an extension of the powers and obligations of local authorities in respect of children in their care and children who are privately fostered.

4. Part I of the Act introduces the changes in the adoption law. These changes follow very closely the recommendations of the Houghton Committee. The Act places the onus on local authorities to ensure the provision of a comprehensive adoption service either by themselves or in conjunction with approved adoption societies. The Secretary of State for Social Services will become responsible for approving voluntary adoption societies.

5. The procedure relating to adoption is reformed and much of the Adoption Act 1958 relating to the effect of adoption orders, eligibility to adopt, domicile, residence, minimum age and marital status is reenacted with modifications. Schedules 1 and 2 set out provisions relating to the effects of adoption on status and property rights in England and Wales and in Scotland. A new procedure is introduced called "freeing a child for adoption" to enable

parents to transfer their parental rights and duties to an adoption agency (which will either be a local authority or an approved adoption society). This will be used as an alternative to the existing procedure for obtaining consent to adoption. The Houghton Committee recommended such a procedure but called this "relinquishment" in their Report. It is hoped that this new procedure will remove the uncertainty which often exists with the present procedure for both natural parents and prospective adopters, as in the latter case any consent to adoption is not final until the adoption application is heard by the court and any question of dispensing with consent cannot be dealt with until then. "Freeing a child for adoption" enables the question of consents to adoption to be finalised before the adoption application hearing.

6. The Act will change the role of the social worker in adoption proceedings, restricting it in one sense and extending it in another. "Welfare supervision" ceases to exist in agency cases and it becomes the responsibility of the placing agency to prepare a report for the court on the suitability of the applicants and other matters. In the case of non-agency placements it will be the task of the local authority social worker to prepare this report. Unlike the 1958 Act procedure where a guardian *ad litem* was always appointed, the new Act provides that a guardian *ad litem* shall be appointed in such cases as are prescribed by rules made under the Act. The guardian *ad litem* will have the duty of safeguarding the interests of the child, again in the manner prescribed by the rules. In future there will be a new officer to assist the court in adoption proceedings and applications to free a child for adoption who will be called a "reporting officer." This officer will assist the court by witnessing agreements to adoption and ensuring that these consents are freely given by parents. Reporting officers and guardians *ad litem* will be selected from a panel of persons established by the Secretary of State.

7. Part I of the Act also introduces certain minor amendments to the law of adoption. Adopted persons over the age of 18 are given the right, which they already have in Scotland, to have access to their birth records and thus to learn the name of their natural parents. Provision is also made for a counselling service to be made available for adopted persons

who seek access to their birth records. If an adopted person under the age of 18 intends to marry he or she is given the right to approach the Registrar General to inquire if the information he has would suggest the person they intend to marry is within the prohibited degrees of relationship. If a foster parent who has looked after the child for five years applies to adopt the child the natural parents will be restricted from removing the child from the foster parents up until the hearing of the application to adopt. The Act also gives adoption agencies the right to make payments in certain circumstances to adopters if the scheme is approved by the Secretary of State.

8. Part II* of the Act introduces the new concept of "custodianship." The Houghton Committee developed the concept of guardianship as a sort of halfway house between fostering and adoption. To avoid confusion with the existing concept of guardianship the Act calls this new status "custodianship," a rather clumsy word to describe the vesting of legal custody in persons, other than the mother or father of the child, who have the child in their care. The local authority will have to be notified of an application for custodianship and prepare a report for the court on the suitability of the applicants and other matters. Custodianship, unlike adoption, is revocable and the court may under section 37* make a custodianship order when an adoption order has been applied for if the court feels that the former order is more appropriate.

9. Part III of the Act contains amendments to the Children Act 1948 and the Children and Young Persons Act 1969, and similar amendments in relation to Scotland to the Social Work (Scotland) Act 1968. Section 1 of the 1948 Act is amended to enable local authorities to require parents to give up to 28 days' notice of their intention to remove a child who has been in care under section 1 for six months or more. This requirement of 28 days' notice is extended to parents intending to remove their child from the care of a voluntary organisation if the child has been in care for six months or more. Section 2 of the 1948 Act (assumption of parental rights by the local authority) is rewritten and extended to include the power to assume parental rights in respect of a child who has been in the care of a local authority for three years or more. Local

authorities are given the right to assume parental rights and duties on behalf of voluntary organisations.

10. Section 1 of the Children and Young Persons Act 1969 is amended to include a new ground for care proceedings where a person who has been convicted of an offence involving violence against a child becomes a member of the same household as any child and is likely to illtreat that child. The court is given power to order separate representation for children in certain proceedings under the Act where it appears that the child's and the parent's interests conflict. Where the court makes such an order it must appoint a guardian *ad litem* to safeguard the interests of the child. Procedures for recovering a child removed from or absconding from care are strengthened.

11. Part IV of the Act explains some of the concepts used in the Act, such as "parental rights and dutes" and "legal custody" and makes further amendments to the law concerning the submitting of reports in guardianship and matrimonial proceedings and the registration of births.

12. Part V of the Act deals with other miscellaneous amendments. The Children Act 1958 which deals with private fostering is amended to empower the Secretary of State to make regulations about this. The Secretary of State is also given power to set up inquiries about children in certain cases. This part of the Act also sets out supplementary provisions relating to the jurisdiction of courts, interpretation and the timing of the implementation of the Act.

13. There is some anxiety, voiced when the Act was still in its Bill form in the House of Lords, that the resources required to implement the provisions of the Act satisfactorily will not be forthcoming so that a situation comparable to that of the Children and Young Persons Act 1969 could arise, with many of the Act's sections remaining unimplemented, or, if brought into force, failing to work through lack of resources.

14. When the Bill was first published the Government appeared to under-estimate the cost of implementing the Act, especially as far as local authorities were concerned. The Government's argument appeared to be that many children in expensive institutional care at present will be freed through the provisions of the Act for fostering or adoption, both economically cheaper. This might well be one of the long term

effects of the Act but it is difficult to see how in the short term it could change the situation where there is a chronic shortage of good residential placements for children. New legislation will not of itself create more foster homes or find more prospective adopters for children who are difficult to place. The short term effects of the Act will be to place yet more statutory obligations on local authorities who are already struggling to cope. For the Act to provide an effective framework within which good child care practices can develop more resources for manpower and training will be needed and more resources for preventive work with parents, otherwise the Act will remain just another piece of legislation which social adminstrators and social workers struggle to implement. For these reasons the implementation of the Act will take place gradually over the next few years as resources become available.

IMPLEMENTATION OF THE ACT

15. Certain provisions which do not involve any cost came into force on the passing of the Act and on January 1, 1976. On the passing of the Act, sections 71 and 72 which give the Secretary of State power to make grants to local authorities in England and Wales and Scotland to provide secure accommodation in community schools, and section 82, which clarifies the powers of reporters to conduct proceedings before a sheriff in Scotland came into force. On January 1, 1976 the following provisions came into force: the new welfare test in adoption proceedings set out in section 3; the new requirement concerning the religious upbringing of a child set out in section 13; the power of the Secretary of State to order inquiries both in England and Wales and Scotland, set out in sections 98 and 99; Schedules 1 and 2 concerning the status of the adopted child and certain other supplementary powers which can be implemented at no extra cost. As a transitional provision the additional ground for dispensing with consent set out in section 12(2)(f)* is added to the existing grounds for dispensing with consent set out in section 5(1) of the Adoption Act 1958 in a new paragraph (c) which takes effect from January 1, 1976. The new paragraph (c) provides that where a

parent has seriously ill-treated the child and that (whether because of the ill-treatment or for other reasons) the rehabilitation of the child within the household of that person is unlikely the court may dispense with parental consent to the adoption.

16. Other minor amendments to the adoption law are likely to be implemented in 1976 and it is hoped that the new provision giving an adopted peson access to his original birth records will be implemented in this period. As the cost of introducing a comprehensive adoption service is estimated to cost an additional £5 million over and above the amount already being spent on adoption it is unlikely that these provisions can be brought in before the financial year 1977-78. The provisions relating to custodianship could not be introduced before 1977-78 either. Dr. David Owen indicated that separate representation for children will be implemented gradually, possibly making a start with applications for the variation and discharge of care or supervision orders under section 21(2) or 15(1) of the Children and Young Persons Act 1969.

17. To enable a consistency of style and to ensure that this book is not out of date within a few months of publication, the book has been written as though all the provisions of the Act have come into force. Those provisions which are not in force, however, by the date of publication have been asterisked to indicate that they have yet to be implemented. All sections of the Act which are not so asterisked are in force.

2 The Provision of an Adoption Service

THE BACKGROUND TO ADOPTION TODAY

18. The Houghton Committee succinctly defines adoption as the "complete severance of the legal relationship between parents and child and the establishment of a new one between the child and his adoptive parents." This severing of the legal relationship between the natural parents and their child is permanent and can only be superseded by a later adoption order.

It was not until this century that the concept of legal adoption was developed in the United Kingdom. Before this informal adoptions were common but did not provide the child concerned with any legal security. The child did not become a part of his "adoptive" family in a legal sense and his situation was comparable to that of a foster child. There was little to stop the natural parents claiming back their child at any time, without any regard being paid to the interests of the child or indeed those of the "adoptive" parents. The First World War left many children fatherless and emphasised the need for a system of legal adoption which provided security for the child and his adoptive family. In 1921 the Hopkinson Committee (Cmd. 1254) was set up to look into this, followed by the two Reports of the Tomlin Committee in 1925 (Cmds. 2401, 2469), which led to the first adoption Act, the Adoption of Children Act 1926 providing for adoption in England and Wales. A similar Act was passed in relation to Scotland in 1930.

19. The initial Acts made legal adoption possible but did not make any legal requirements or set standards for adoption agencies. Following the report of the Horsburgh Committee (Cmd. 5499), the Adoption of Children (Regulation) Act was passed in 1939 to ensure the compulsory registration of

adoption societies and to make regulations for the placement
of children with a view to adoption. The Adoption Act 1949
made further changes which together with the other Adoption
Acts was consolidated in the Adoption Act 1950. The next
major Act in this field, the Adoption Act 1958, which
implemented most of the Hurst Committee's recommendations
(Cmd. 9248) has remained the governing Act, but many of its
provisions will be repealed and amended by the Childrens Act
1975. The Houghton Committee was set up in 1969 to consider
again the law, policy and procedure on the adoption of
children, and the 1975 Act is based on many of its
recommendations. In spite of the relatively short history of the
law of adoption there has been a constant process of change
and amendment reflecting the growth of knowledge in this
field and the changing role of adoption in our society.

Since 1926 the development of the adoption service
throughout the country has been piecemeal and unco-
ordinated. Voluntary societies and agencies responsible for
adoption grew up following the 1926 Act but some areas of the
country received better coverage than others, and the services
and resources which each society offered varied immensely.
Adoption was well established as a service when children's
departments were first set up in 1948 and this seems to have led
to a situation where adoption was not always amongst the
range of services which local authorities provided for children.

20. Before the 1975 Act local authorities had the option of
acting as adoption agencies. At the time of the Houghton
Committee 96 local authorities in England and Wales out of a
total of 172 acted as adoption agencies, again leading to great
variations throughout the country in the availability and
quality of the adoption service. The splitting of adoption
services from the usual child care services provided by
children's departments in many local authorities, a split which
as we have seen developed historically, seems to be partly
responsible for the situation which has grown up in local
authorities where adoption is rarely considered as an
alternative for children in long term care, even for those with
no parental contact. This is so despite the fact that research
has shown the value of adoption as a form of substitute care for
a child and the advantages it has for many children over both
residential and foster care.

THE ESTABLISHMENT OF A COMPREHENSIVE
ADOPTION SERVICE

21. The Houghton Committee found that there was a continuing need for an adoption service and felt that it should be available throughout the country as part of a comprehensive social work service for children and families. They recommended that local authorities should be required by law to ensure that an adoption service is provided within their area and this is given effect by section 1* of the Act.

Section 1(1)* provides that:

"It is the duty of every local authority to establish and maintain within their area a service designed to meet the needs, in relation to adoption, of —

    (*a*) children who have been or may be adopted,

    (*b*) parents and guardians of such children, and

    (*c*) persons who have adopted or may adopt a child,

and for that purpose to provide the requisite facilities, or secure that they are provided by approved adoption societies."

The "requisite facilities" to be provided are, as subsection (2)* lists:

"(*a*) temporary board and lodging where needed by pregnant women, mothers or children;

 (*b*) arrangements for assessing children and prospective adopters, and placing children for adoption;

 (*c*) counselling for persons with problems relating to adoption."

The range of services which section 1* indicates the adoption agency should provide is very broadly drawn. For example, "counselling for persons with problems relating to adoption" could be interpreted very widely and would include counselling childless couples. In a situation of scarce resources it is clear that certain of these services such as placement of children will be given priority whilst counselling of childless couples would almost certainly come lower down the list. But it is clear that it will not be sufficient for an agency to act as a placement agency only and it will have to be able to draw on a much wider range of resources if it is to be approved. Many adoption societies will not have this range of resources but they may provide a service in conjunction with the local authority, so that help may be given in a co-ordinated manner without duplication, omission or avoidable delay" (section 1(3)*). Section 1(3)* stresses that the facilities provided under subsection (1)* must be provided in conjunction with the local authority's other social services. Concern was expressed before the Act was passed that it might cause local authorities to give the adoption service too much prominence as against the other services they provided for families and children, in spite of the provisions of section 1(3)*. Because of this section 2* was introduced into the Act which sets adoption within the context of the other social services which the local authority provides for children. The section adds nothing to the existing duties of local authorities but should prevent an imbalance growing up between resources allocated to the adoption service and the other services for children provided by local authorities.

THE APPROVAL OF ADOPTION AGENCIES

22. It was not until 1939 that any provision was made for the regulation of voluntary adoption societies. A system of control was then developed in the form of registration whereby voluntary adoption societies had to register with the local authority within whose area their offices were situated. The procedure was open to many criticisms largely because of the differences in the exercise of these powers by local authorities and the narrowness of the criteria laid down for registration. In line with the Houghton Committee's recommendations the 1975 Act transfers responsibility to central government for the approval of adoption societies. Section 4(1)* lays down that:

"A body desiring to act as an adoption society or, if it is already an adoption society, desiring to continue to act as such in England and Wales or in Scotland may, in the manner specified by regulations made by the Secretary of State, apply to the Secretary of State for his approval to its doing so."

These regulations have yet to be drafted but subsections (3)* to (5)* of section 4* specify what matters will be taken into account. The Secretary of State has to have regard to —

"(a) the applicant's adoption programme, including, in particular, its ability to make provision for children

who are free for adoption,
- (*b*) the number and qualifications of its staff,
- (*c*) its financial resources, and
- (*d*) the organisation and control of its operations.'
(subs.(3)*).

Subsection (4)* requires the Secretary of State, if the applicant is likely to operate extensively within the area of a particular local authority, to ask the authority whether they support the application and to take into account any views about it that the authority may put to him. Subsection (5)* provides that where, either before or after the passing of the Act, the applicant is already acting as an adoption society or is already an approved adoption society, the Secretary of State shall have regard to the record and reputation of the applicant and the areas within which and the scale on which it is currently operating or has operated in the past.

23. Subsection (2)* provides more generally that besides subsections (3)* to (5)* the Secretary of State may have regard to "other relevant considerations" and then if "he is satisfied that the applicant is likely to make, or, if the applicant is an approved adoption society, is making an effective contribution to the Adoption Service, or, as the case may be, to the Scottish Adoption Service" he shall give his approval, which will be effective from the date specified in the notice of approval, or in the case of renewal of approval from the date of the notice. Approval under section 4* lasts for 3 years from the date upon which it becomes operative unless it is renewed by a further application under subsection (1)* or is withdrawn earlier by the Secretary of State (subs.(7)*). The Secretary of State has power to refuse an application for approval if he is not satisfied that the society is likely to make, or is making an effective contribution to the Adoption Service, and this must be given by notice in writing and is subject to the procedure set out in section 6(1)* and (2)* (subs.(6)*).

24. Section 5* empowers the Secretary of State to withdraw approval from a body approved under section 4* by notice from a date specified in the notice, if it appears that "the body is not making an effective contribution to the Adoption Service." Under section 5(2)* he is empowered to withdraw approval from an approved adoption society which fails to

provide him with information which he requires to carry out his functions under section 5(1)* or fails to verify such information in the manner required by him. He is empowered to make arrangements for children who are in the care of a body whose approval is withdrawn under subsections (1)* and (2)* and for any other transitional matters which may in the circumstances appear to him to be necessary (subs. (3)*).

25. The procedure which the Secretary of State must observe on refusing to approve an adoption society or withdrawing approval from an adoption society is set out in section 6*. If the Secretary of State has decided to refuse an application for approval in accordance with section 4(6)* he must first serve on the applicant a notice setting out the reasons why he proposes to refuse the application and informing the applicant that the society has 28 days from the service of the notice to make representations to him. The Secretary of State then has to take into account any representations which are made before reaching his final decision (subs.(2)*). Subsections (3)* and (4)* set out a similar procedure in relation to withdrawal of approval. Once the Secretary of State has carried out this procedure as set out in section 6* and has considered any representations made to him, but still feels that approval should be refused or withdrawn then he may refuse approval in accordance with section 4(6)* or withdraw approval in accordance with section 5(1)*.

26. If an approved adoption society has become inactive or defunct, the Secretary of State may direct in relation to any child who is or was in the care of the society that the appropriate local authority should take any such action as the society might have taken; and if the local authority is not automatically entitled as of right to take this action then rights to enable the local authority to do this are temporarily granted in this respect by section 7(1)*. Before any direction is made under section 7(1)* by the Secretary of State he must, if practicable, consult with both the society and the local authority involved (subs.(2)*).

27. How the quality of service provided by a local authority acting as an adoption agency can be controlled was the subject of much discussion in the House of Lords at the Committee stage of the Bill. The approval procedure laid down in section

4* cannot be applied to local authorities as such a requiremen
would be inconsistent with the duty which is laid upon them b
section 1* to provide an adoption service. Nonetheless i
cannot be denied that the standards between one loca
authority and another can vary enormously. Nowadays th
Social Work Service of the Department of Health and Socia
Security advises local authorities on the promotion an
maintenance of standards rather than acting as a
inspectorate as it did in the days of the children's departments
Many of their Lordships regretted this shift of emphasis an
the strength of their feelings that standards should be set fo
local authorities in the adoption and child care field in genera
indicates that there may be moves in the future to bring bac
the use of the Social Work Service's inspectorial powers. Th
disparity between local authority standards in relation t
adoption will not be resolved by merely resuscitatin
"inspection". If higher standards are to be achieved the nee
for greater resources to be allocated to local authorities is onc
again underlined.

The Effects of an Adoption Order

This chapter examines the effects of an adoption order first from the adoptive parent's point of view and secondly from the adoptive child's.

28. The effects of an adoption order were defined statutorily by sections 13 to 19 of the Adoption Act 1958 and although the new Act largely replaces these sections it does not introduce any major changes in this respect. Section 8(1)* of the Act states the general definition of an adoption order:

"An adoption order is an order vesting the parental rights and duties relating to a child in the adopters, made on their application by an authorised court."

A "child" is defined in the Act as a person under the age of 18 (section 107(1)). The definition of an "authorised court" is set out in section 100. At present the tripartite division of jurisdiction over adoption cases remains between the High Court, the county court and the magistrates' court, but in the magistrates' court an application will no longer be heard by the juvenile court but by the magistrates' court which deals with domestic proceedings. These magistrates do not have specialist training in court work involving children at present, unlike the magistrates who sit in the juvenile court, and presumably some training scheme will have to be instituted for them if standards are to be maintained. In place of this division of jurisdiction between three courts the Houghton Committee suggested that a system of family courts should be set up. This would enable judges and magistrates to develop specialist skills in dealing with family matters. The Govenment is now committed to introduce family courts eventually which means that the definition of "authorised court" is likely to be amended in the future.

WHAT PARENTAL RIGHTS AND DUTIES
DOES AN ADOPTION ORDER CONFER?

29. The concept of parental rights and duties is used throughout the Act but seems to evade precise legal definition. The concept consists of a collection of rights and duties, the most obvious of which are the right to custody, care, maintenance, to make decisions concerning the child's education, religion, health and so on. Section 8(1)* of the Act embodies the general principle previously set out in section 13 of the 1958 Act that all parental rights and duties are vested in the adopters. Section 8(3)* of the 1975 Act makes it clear that an adoption order extinguishes from the time of the making of the order any parental rights and duties which were vested in any parent or guardian, or in any person by virtue of a court order. Thus, for example, an adoption order automatically extinguishes a previously granted custody order in favour of one parent as against the other, an order under the Guardianship of Minors Act 1971, or a care order to a local authority. It also follows that just as a custody order is extinguished in these circumstances so a right of access granted to the other natural parent is lost. A resolution assuming parental rights in respect of a child made by a local authority under section 2 of the Children Act 1948 ceases to have effect upon the making of a subsequent adoption order (section 2(8)* of the 1948 Act as amended by the 1975 Act in relation to England and Wales, section 16(9)* of the Social Work (Scotland) Act 1968 as amended by the 1975 Act in relation to Scotland).

30. The vesting of the natural parents' rights in relation to education, the appointment of a guardian and consent to marriage in the adoptive parents is not specifically mentioned as it is in section 13 of the 1958 Act, but these rights are automatically transferred by section 8(1)* of the 1975 Act. Legislation relating to taxation, pension schemes, and social security provisions may make specific reference to the position of the adopted child, but where this is not the case the Act makes it clear that the adopted child is to be treated, in the case of married adopters, as if he had been born a child of their marriage (irrespective of whether he had been born

before the couple had married or not) or, in the case of a single
adopter, as a legitimate child born in wedlock but not of any
actual marriage (Schedule 1, para. 3 in relation to England
and Wales, Schedule 2, para. 1 in relation to Scotland).

31. Where there is a duty to make maintenance payments in
respect of a child either because of an agreement or because of
a court order, this duty ceases on the making of an adoption
order (section 8(3)(*b*)*). This does not however prejudice the
right to recover any arrears due under an agreement or order
up until the time when the adoption order was made. There
are two cases however where this duty to make payments will
not be extinguished: first, where the agreement to make a
payment constitutes a trust; and secondly, in cases where the
agreement contains an express provision that the duty is not to
be extinguished by the making of an adoption order (section
8(4)*). The 1974 Act repeals the exception to the rule that an
adoption order extinguishes an affiliation order except in the
case of a single woman who adopted her own child, with the
effect that an affiliation order is always brought to an end by
an adoption order (Schedule 4, Part 1).

32. The concept of parental rights and duties which is used
in section 8(1)* in the definition of an adoption order and
throughout the Act is explained in section 85. This provides
that parental rights and duties means "as respects a particular
child)(whether legitimate or not), all the rights and duties
which by law the mother and father have in relation to a
legitimate child and his property;..." Apart from the
exceptional circumstances of a separation agreement between
husband and wife which is possible under section 1(2) of the
Guardianship Act 1973 it is not possible for a person to
surrender or transfer to another any parental right or duty
which he has in relation to a child (section 85(2)). This is not a
new principle and was previously embodied in the common
law. Where parental rights and duties are held jointly by two
or more persons any one of them may exercise them in any way
provided that the other(s) have not signified disapproval
(section 85(3)). Where parental rights and duties are held
jointly by two or more persons and one person dies the rights
and duties vest in the survivor(s) (section 85(4)). On the death
of a person having parental rights and duties exclusively those

rights and duties lapse, but they may be acquired by another
person at any time under any enactment (section 85(5)).
Subsections (4) and (5) apply in relation to the dissolution of a
body corporate as they apply to the death of an individual
(subs.(6)). As before, in the case of an illegitimate child the
mother has exclusive parental rights and duties during her
lifetime unless otherwise provided by or under any other
enactment (subs.(7)).

WHAT RIGHTS DOES AN ADOPTION ORDER CONFER ON THE ADOPTED CHILD?

33. As outlined above the Act confers on adopted children
the legal status of children born into the adopted family
(Schedule 1, para. 3 in relation to England and Wales,
Schedule 2, para. 1 in relation to Scotland). These provisions
make it clear that an adopted child cannot be illegitimate
following the recommendations of the Houghton Committee.
The provisions of the 1958 Act were less clear-cut on this point
and only provided for a transfer of parental rights and duties
for certain purposes. This transfer of the adopted child
completely into his adopted family has meant changes being
made to the laws of inheritance and legitimation on this point
and these are set out in the first two Schedules to the Act.

34. The provisions of Schedule 1 apply not only to adoption
orders made under current or previous adoption law in
England and Wales but also to orders made in Northern
Ireland, the Isle of Man, the Channel Islands and any order
made abroad which is recognised here under section 4(3) of the
Adoption Act 1958. Section 16 of the 1958 Act previously
governed the position of adopted children in the construction
of wills and provided that in the case of wills executed before
the adoption order was made the adopted child could not
benefit. The 1975 Act provides that in the case of wills
executed after January 1, 1976, all adopted children will
benefit as if they were children of the family unless the testator
indicates a contrary intention. Those who have already been
adopted acquire this new status from January 1, 1976, and, in
the case of subsequent adoptions, from the date of the
adoption. Schedule 1 contains provisions to ensure that an
illegitimate child who is subsequently adopted by one or both

of his parents does not lose any property rights through being adopted. Part III of Schedule 1 introduces changes in relation to the property rights of legitimated children similar to those introduced for adopted children. Schedule 2 sets out these new provisions in relation to Scotland. This had to be drafted separately because of the separate statutory provisions which relate to the law of inheritance and legitimation in Scotland.

35. There are two ways in which the legal position of the adopted child remains different from that of a child born into the family. The first concerns the laws relating to marriage and incest. The Houghton Committee discussed whether a person may marry his relations by adoption if they did not otherwise fall within the prohibited degrees of relationship (which are set out in the table of kindred and affinity in Schedule 1 to the Marriage Act 1949). Under the 1958 Act the adopter and the adopted child are deemed to fall within the prohibited degrees of relationship but an adopted person may otherwise marry a relation by adoption. Despite the adoption order the adopted child is prohibited from marrying his natural relatives who fall within the prohibited degrees. The Law Commission for England and Wales favoured leaving the law unchanged when it considered this point, but the Kilbrandon Committee on the Law of Marriage in Scotland favoured an extension on the law in this respect to include adoptive brothers and sisters and adoptive nephews and nieces within the prohibited degrees. The Houghton Committee felt, on balance, that the current restrictions should not be extended and this view has prevailed. Thus paragraph 7 of Schedule 1 provides that in relation to his relatives by adoption an adopted child does not fall within the prohibited degrees of marriage. Neither do the laws relating to incest (set out in sections 10 and 11 of the Sexual Offences Act 1956) apply to him in relation to his relatives by adoption. Similar provisions apply to adopted children in Scotland except that a child and his adopter are deemed to be within the prohibited degrees of marriage (Schedule 2, para. 1(3)).

36. Again the adopted child is placed in a different position from a child born into a family in that he cannot inherit any title of honour, peerage or dignity either in England and Wales or Scotland, a subject of some discussion when the Act

was in its Bill form in the House of Lords, but a provision
which will not affect the majority of adopted children
(Schedule 1, para. 10 in relation to England and Wales,
Schedule 2, para. 5(4) in relation to Scotland).

37. The Act extends the rights of adopted persons by giving
them the right on attaining the age of 18 to obtain a copy of
their original birth certificate in accordance with the
recommendations of the Houghton Committee (section 26* of
the Act amending section 20 of the 1958 Act and inserting a
new section 20A* into that Act). This will bring England and
Wales into line with Scotland where the right already exists for
an adopted child to obtain a copy of his original birth
certificate (but at the age of 17 not 18 as in the new provisions
relating to England and Wales). Before this it was not
impossible for an adopted person to obtain access to his
original birth certificate. Section 20(5) of the 1958 Act
provides that the adopted person could make an application to
the High Court, the Westminster County Court, or the court
which make the adoption order to have access to his birth
records. Such orders are rarely granted. If an adopted person
knows his original name however there is nothing to prevent
him applying to Somerset House for a copy of his original birth
certificate. Adoptive parents are usually aware of the adopted
child's original name, as the original birth certificate would
have been lodged at the court together with the other papers
when the parents first made the adoption application.

38. The Houghton Committee before making this
recommendation considered a study made by Dr. J. Triseliotis
in Scotland of adopted persons who had sought access to their
birth records (just over 40 a year on average). Dr. Triseliotis
found that where an adopted person has been told of his
adoption at an early age and has a good relationship with his
adopters he is less likely to seek access to his original birth
records. Significantly, only two-fifths of those applying for
access to their original birth records had been told of their
adoption, the rest having found out by chance from other
sources that they were adopted. The application for
information seems to have been triggered in many cases by the
death of one of the adoptive parents or the approaching
marriage of the adopted person. Two-thirds of those who had

sought this information felt it was of some help to them, but one-third felt upset by the information they had obtained. Nevertheless, on being interviewed four months later 9 out of 10 had no regrets at having sought this information. The number of persons who, having gained access to their original birth records, sought to contact their natural parents was about 60 per cent. of the sample (42 out of 70 people) and only 4 succeeded in doing so although 7 others managed to contact blood relatives. There was no record at Register House (the Scottish equivalent of Somerset House) of any complaint being made by a natural parent who had been traced by an adopted person having access to their records.

39. Dr. Triseliotis's study indicates that the new right conferred on the adopted person by section 26* of the Act will probably be used relatively rarely. The likelihood of tracing natural parents from the original birth records seems remote as the mother is likely to have moved from the address shown on the birth certificate. Thus the threat that this new provision will pose to natural parents who would prefer that their children did not try to contact them is not a great one. What Dr. Triseliotis's study highlights is the adopted child's basic need for information about his natural family rather than just access to his birth records. Where a child has been told of his adoption at an early age and has a good relationship with his adopters he is less likely to seek access to his birth records. Children who learn of their adoption in less happy ways are likely to need more help than the mere sight of their original birth certificate. As the Houghton Committee pointed out there is a need for skilled help and counselling for many adopted persons who feel the need to try to trace their origins. Many agencies make it part of their practice to help adopted persons in this way but some adopted persons may not be told which agency was responsible for placing them. The Committee recommended that the name of the adoption agency should appear on the adoption order and that adoption records should be preserved for 75 years to enable the adopted person to go back to the agency for help in this respect. The new section 20A* inserted into the 1958 Act by section 26* of the 1975 Act provides that the Registrar General, each local authority and each approved adoption society must provide a

counselling service for adopted persons who apply for their original birth records (subs. (3)*). Before supplying the applicant with his original birth certificate the Registrar General has a duty to inform the applicant that there are counselling services available to him either at the General Register Office, from the local authority for the area where the applicant is at the time of the application, from the local authority for the area where the court sat which made the original adoption order, or if the adoption was arranged by an approved adoption society from that society (subs. (4)*). If the applicant chooses to receive counselling from a local authority or an approved adoption society the Registrar General must send the details of the original birth entry to them (subs. (5)*). If the applicant was adopted before the 1975 Act was passed the Registrar General has a duty not to supply the details of the original birth entry unless the person has attended an interview with a counsellor at the General Register Office or with an officer of the local authority or of an adoption society in accordance with subsection (4)* (subs. (6)*). As section 20A* of the 1958 Act only applies to England and Wales, section 27* of the 1975 Act amends section 22 of the 1958 Act to make similar provision for Scotland. In this case however the counselling duties fall on the local authority and approved adoption agencies only and not on the Registrar General for Scotland. As the right to apply for the original birth certificate existed before the 1975 Act there is no requirement in Scotland that a person adopted before the 1975 Act was passed must have an interview with a counsellor before information can be given. It is envisaged that the numbers of people requiring counselling of this nature will be very small, and that counsellors will be social workers.

40. The new section 20A* of the 1958 Act gives an adopted child who is under 18 but planning to marry, the right to approach the Registrar General to see if it appears to him from the birth records or other information that he has whether the applicant and the person he intends to marry will come within the prohibited degrees of relationship for the purposes of marriage (section 20A(2)*) of the 1958 Act as inserted by the 1975 Act). This is necessary as although adopted children may marry adoptive relatives within the prohibited degrees of

marriage except their adopter they may not marry natural relatives who fall within the prohibited degrees.

4 The Making of an Adoption Order

THE GUIDING PRINCIPLE IN ADOPTION PROCEEDINGS

41. The guiding principle for a court or adoption agency in any proceedings relating to the adoption of a child is set out in section 3 of the 1975 Act and represents one of the most important changes that the Act introduces. Section 3 provides that:

"In reaching any decision relating to the adoption of a child, a court or adoption agency shall have regard to all the circumstances, first consideration being given to the need to safeguard and promote the welfare of the child throughout his childhood; and shall so far as practicable ascertain the wishes and feelings of the child regarding the decision and give due consideration to them, having regard to his age and understanding."

This replaces the "welfare test" which was set out in section 7(1)(*b*) of the Adoption Act 1958 which provided that:

"The court before making an adoption order shall be satisfied —

(*b*) that the order if made will be for the welfare of the infant;"

This test gave the court no indication as to how a conflict of interests between, child, natural parents and prospective adopters should be resolved.

42. The new welfare test which is set out in section 3 strengthens the position of the child considerably and ensures that the court or adoption agency takes into account the wishes of the child, something which is usually done if this is at all practicable, but has not been required by law before. Before the new Act much concern had been expressed that in adoption proceedings the governing principle the court had to

take into account before reaching any decision was different from that in guardianship and custody proceedings, where the principle was that the welfare of the child should be "the first and paramount consideration." In the Houghton Committee's Working Paper which was published before their Report the Committee suggested that the welfare of the child should be the "first and paramount consideration" in adoption proceedings as in custody and guardianship. However after the publication of the Working Paper an important case in adoption law decided by the House of Lords, *Re W.* ([1971] A.C.682), made it quite clear that in a contested adoption case where there was an application to dispense with consent on the grounds that the mother was withholding her consent unreasonably the court has to take into account the welfare of the child when making their decision. The Houghton Committee's Report which was published after this case pointed out that if the child's welfare were declared to be the "first and paramount" consideration this would be incompatible with the test of whether a parent was withholding consent unreasonably, as paramount means that the child's welfare is the overriding consideration in every case.

43. There was also some anxiety that if what has become known as the "paramountcy" principle were introduced into adoption proceedings natural parents might be penalised as against prospective adopters who could offer the child greater material benefits and social status. The Houghton Committee eventually recommended that the welfare of the child should be the "first consideration" but not the paramount consideration. This recommendation was not however followed when the Bill was first introduced into the House of Lords. Section 3 as it then stood introduced a new test of "taking full account of the need to safeguard and promote the welfare of the child throughout his childhood." Many of their Lordships felt that this was an "insipid" test and the concept of the child's welfare being the first consideration was introduced as an amendment. There was some concern that such an amendment could introduce difficulties in judicial decision-making as no guidelines are given as to what are the second and third considerations, for example, but the amendment was accepted after a division. The new welfare test represents a

compromise between the two extremes of the paramountcy test which could swing the balance against the natural parents too far and the "long-term welfare" test which their Lordships felt did not safeguard the child's interests sufficiently. But until the courts have begun to interpret "first consideration" and a body of case law has been built up around this it is difficult to predict the impact which this change will have on the decisions of courts in adoption proceedings. The new test will however be especially important in relation to the question of consents to adoption which is discussed in Chapter 5.

WHO MAY ADOPT

44. There are relatively few legal criteria with which adopters have to comply to be eligible to adopt and the Houghton Committee felt that this was as it should be. They felt that the critical decisions as to the placement of children were best left to the adoption agency for the applicant's suitability to be assessed by the agency in each individual case. Certain basic conditions are laid down by statute and they are re-enacted in the 1975 Act with some modifications. These requirements are:

(a) *Domicile*

45. Domicile is a complex legal concept, which, grossly over-simplified, means the country which a person chooses as their permanent home and where in fact they reside, or, in the absence of such choice, the domicile of his father at the time of the person's birth. It is not dependent on nationality or even on "residence" in a country although a person will usually be both domiciled and resident in the same country. The 1958 Adoption Act laid down requirements for prospective adopters both in terms of domicile and residence in a country within the United Kingdom. The 1975 Act simplifies this in that it only uses the concept of domicile and does not specifically require residence in a country, although the two usually coincide. Thus, in the case of a married couple, the Act (section 10(2)*) requires that one of the couple must be domiciled in a party of the United Kingdom, or in the Channel Islands, or the Isle of

Man, or the application must be for a Convention adoption order (see Chapter 7) before an order can be made. In the case of a single person applying to adopt he must be domiciled in a part of the United Kingdom, or in the Channel Islands, or the Isle of Man, or must be applying for a Convention adoption order before an order can be granted (section 11(2)*).

(b) *Age of the applicants*

The 1975 Act changes the minimum age requirements for adopters which were previously laid down by the 1958 Act in accordance with the recommendations of the Houghton Committee. Now, in the case of a married couple who are applying to adopt each must have attained the age of 21 (section 10(1)*). A single person who applies to adopt must also have attained the age of 21 (section 11(1)*).

(c) *Marital status*

(i) Married couples

47. Only a married couple may adopt jointly; two or more other persons cannot make a joint adoption application (section 10(1)*). Thus a couple who have cohabited for many years but who are not married cannot make a joint application to adopt.

Joint applications by parent and step-parent to adopt. The Houghton Committee gave careful consideration to the growing numbers of adoptions by parent and step-parent. In 1970, for example, 5,202 legitimate children and 5,054 illegitimate children were adopted in England and Wales by a parent and step-parent. The reason for this large number of adoptions seems to be that by adoption the step-parent can show that he or she completely accepts the child of the other spouse into the new family unit, the child's name and birth certificate are changed and the step-parent acquires jointly with the other spouse the full legal rights and obligations in respect of the child. The Committee were critical of this practice in that such adoptions cut off the child from one side of his natural family. For example, if the natural parents are divorced and the mother later remarries and she and her new husband apply to adopt the child of her first marriage, the natural father, the paternal grandparents, aunts, uncles and so on cease to be legally related to the child. The natural father's right of access ceases. It was also felt that if adoption were used in this way it might conceal from the child the reality of his family background, and this in itself could be harmful. The Committee felt that whilst there was a difference between legitimate and illegitimate children adopted jointly in this way it would be invidious to distinguish between the two and adoptions by parent and step-parent should be allowed in exceptional circumstances only in both cases. The Act gives effect to this recommendation in two ways. First, section 10(3)* provides that where a step-parent and parent apply to the court to adopt the court must dismiss the application if it considers that the matter would be better dealt with by the custody order made at the time of the divorce being varied. This does not offer a very attractive alternative to such parents who would have to return to the domestic court which made the original custody order for a variation of that order. The step-parent does not acquire exclusive rights in these circumstances and neither would the child's name be changed. Where there is no divorce but the parent and step-parent of an illegitimate child apply to adopt that child the court may, if it feels the new status of custodianship (discussed in Chapter 8) is more appropriate, grant a custodianship order instead of an adoption order (section 37* in relation to England and Wales, section 53* in relation to Scotland).

(ii) Single adopters

48. The prohibition of an adoption of a female child by a single male applicant laid down by the 1958 Act is repealed by the new Act*, and single adopters of either sex may now apply. If however the applicant is married the court can only consider an application from him alone if the court is satisfied that the other spouse cannot be found, or the spouses have separated and are living apart and their separation is likely to be permanent, or one spouse because of either physical or mental ill health is incapable of making an adoption application

(section 11(1)*). If the application for the adoption order is by
the mother or the father of the child alone the court must be
satisfied that either the other natural parent is dead or cannot
be found or that there is some reason to justify the exclusion of
the other natural parent. If the court makes an order in these
circumstances it must record the reason justifying the
exclusion of the other natural parent (section 11(3)*). Thus
applications to adopt by a single parent will be relatively rare.
The court must dismiss an application by a step-parent alone
(which would, of course, extinguish the rights of both natural
parents) if the child has already been named in proceedings in
the matrimonial courts and the court feels the matter would be
better dealt with by a variation of custody order (section
11(4)*). In these circumstances the court will not be
empowered to make a custodianship order (see Chapter 8).

(d) *The suitability of the applicants*

49. Under the 1958 Act procedure there is a period of three
months prior to the adoption application during which the
child is placed with the applicants, who are supported and
helped with problems related to the settling in of the child by
an officer of the local authority. This is called "welfare
supervision." The Houghton committee considered this to be
valuable but wondered if a social worker from an adoption
agency were already involved if this was not a duplication of
work. The new Act brings "welfare supervision" in agency
cases to an end. It also changes the role of the guardian *ad
litem*, whose job under the 1958 Act procedure was to prepare
a report for the court on, amongst other things, the suitability
of the applicants. This task is now left to the adoption agency,
or in the case where an adoption agency is not involved, the
local authority where the applicant lives (section 22(3)*,
section 18)2)*). The court must be satisfied that sufficient
opportunities to see the child with the applicant or applicants
in their home environment have been afforded to the adoption
agency, or in a non-agency case, to the local authority within
whose area the applicant(s) has his home (section 9(3)*).

WHO MAY BE ADOPTED

50. Only a child, that is a person under the age of 18, may be adopted. An adoption order may not be made however if the child is, or has been, married (section 8(5)*). There is nothing to prevent a child who has been adopted being the subject of a new adoption application (section 8(8)*).

WHO MAY ARRANGE ADOPTIONS

51. Adoptions by non-relatives are most frequently arranged by adoption agencies. A small number of adoptions however are arranged by third parties who, for one reason or another, know of a child available for adoption and know of a couple who wish to adopt. The couple may even approach the natural parent directly and so the matter is arranged. Such placements have always aroused some concern. The criteria by which the suitability of adopters is assessed are, as we have seen, not specifically laid down by statute for the most part. It is adoption agencies who have built up a body of knowledge and expertise in relation to assessing the suitability of prospective adopters. They are experts in this field and have as their guiding principle the welfare of the child. This may not always be so with third party placements of children, where considerations such as a childless couple's desire for a child, or the natural mother's wish to hush up the birth of a child may prevail over the long term interests of the child. The Houghton Committee felt that:

"Adoption is a matter of such importance to the child (who is usually too young to have any say in the matter) that society has a duty to ensure that the most satisfactory placements are made. Society manifestly does not do so where it is open to anybody to place a child for adoption."

Although the court hearing may act as a final safeguard it was felt that the child's interests need protecting at an earlier stage and they recommended that third party placements should be made illegal. Section 28* of the new Act amending section 29 of the 1958 Act gives effect to this recommendation. Subsection (1)* as amended reads:

"A person other than an adoption agency shall not make

arrangements for the adoption of a child, or place a child for adoption, unless —
  (a) the proposed adopter is a relative of the child, or
  (b) he is acting in pursuance of an order of the High Court."

It becomes an offence to contravene subsection (1)* which is punishable by a term of imprisonment not exceeding three months or a fine not exceeding £400 or both. It also becomes an offence to receive a child placed in contravention of subsection (1)* which is subject to the same penalties. Despite this it still remains technically possible for a person to apply for an adoption order who had a child placed with him by a third party provided that the child has lived with the applicant for 12 months prior to the application (section 9(2)*). Whilst being aware that this could be used as a possible loophole in the law prohibiting third party placements, Dr David Owen expressed the view in the House of Commons that the period of one year and the penalties for contravening section 21(1)* should deter such placements.

Payments to adopters by adoption agencies

52. Payments in relation to adoptions are prohibited by section 50 of the 1958 Adoption Act, whether they be to facilitate the adoption of a child by a person, the granting of consent, the transfer of care and possession of a child with a view to adoption, or the making by a person of any arrangements for the adoption of a child. The Houghton Committee felt however that there might be a case for making payments to adopters in certain circumstances. It was felt that more homes might be found for handicapped children if there were some scheme of payments. Equally there might be children in long term foster care whose foster parents would like to adopt to give them legal security but who need the financial security of their boarding out allowance. On the other side of the coin it was felt to be wrong to subsidise adoptive parents in this way with financial help which, had it been available to the natural parents, would have obviated the need for adoption. On balance the Houghton Committee felt there should be some research and experimentation into

schemes of payment for adoptive parents. Section 32* of the
Act introduces the power for adoption agencies to make
payments to adopters. The agency must submit the proposed
scheme to the Secretary of State for his approval, and he has
power at any time to make alterations to the scheme or to
revoke it (section 50(5) of the 1958 Act as amended by section
32* of the 1975 Act). This power is only likely to be used in
exceptional circumstances and such schemes of payments will
probably only be set up for the adopters of children with
special difficulties. Subsection (6)* lays a duty on the Secretary
of State to report within seven years of the date on which this
section comes into force on the operation of such schemes, and
to report thereafter at five yearly intervals.

5   Consents to Adoption

Section 12* of the new Act replaces section 4 of the 1958 Act in relation to consents to adoption. This section sets out what consents are required and on what grounds consent may be dispensed with. In this chapter what consents are required, the new procedure of freeing a child for adoption and dispensing with consent are examined.

WHAT CONSENTS ARE REQUIRED?

53. The consent of each parent or guardian to an adoption is still required by the new Act as in the 1958 Act, although the 1975 Act uses the word "agreement" rather than "consent." Section 12(1)* of the Act provides that:

"An adoption order shall not be made unless —

(a) the child is free for adoption; or

(b) in the case of each parent or guardian the court is satisfied that —

(i) he freely, and with full understanding of what is involved, agrees unconditionally to the making of the adoption order (whether or not he knows the identity of the applicants), or

(ii) his agreement to the making of the adoption order should be dispensed with on a ground specified in subsection (2)."

The term "parent" in the 1958 Act was held not to include a putative father (in *Re M. (An Infant)* [1955] 2Q.B. 479) and this would still apply. Even if a parent is under the age of 18 he or she still has the right to consent to the adoption of a child. Any agreement to adoption which is made by the mother less than six weeks after the birth of a child is ineffective (section 12(4)*).

54. In England and Wales the child does not have the right

to consent to his adoption, although the new welfare test set
out in section 3 requires the court and the adoption agency to
ascertain the wishes and feelings of the child, having regard to
his age and understanding. In Scotland a child who is a minor
(that is a girl of 12 years or over, or a boy of 14 or over, up to
18) has to consent to the adoption order before it can be made.
This right is preserved for minors in Scotland in section 8(6)*,
and an adoption order can only be made in Scotland in respect
of a minor, if the minor consents to the order or the court is
satisfied that he is incapable of giving his consent.

FREEING A CHILD FOR ADOPTION

55. Although the consent procedure which is currently in
use remains, the 1975 Act introduces an alternative procedure
called "freeing a child for adoption." The question of parental
consent to adoption was reviewed by the Houghton Committee
and they felt that the timing of the existing consent procedure
had many disadvantages. Because the parent has to consent to
a specific adoption and because parental rights and duties
cannot be left in limbo, the transfer of these rights could not
take place until the actual adoption hearing. Thus, although
the natural parent will have signed a consent form shortly
before the adoption application is made, the parental rights
and duties in respect of the child remain vested in him until
the granting of the adoption order. The prospective adopters
often find that the period leading up to the adoption hearing is
a very anxious one for them, as they fear that the natural
parent will withdraw consent before the adoption hearing.
Similarly the natural parents are under great strain
throughout the period leading up to the adoption as they know
they have not made an irrevocable decision until the adoption
application has been granted. Research has shown how
difficult this period can be for mothers who have placed their
children for adoption (J. Triseliotis and C. Hall, "Giving
consent to adoption," *Social Work Today*, December 2,
1971.). Equally if an older child has been placed for adoption
this can be a very anxious period for him also.

56. Because of these disadvantages the Houghton Committee gave consideration to some system of "relinquishment" of

Freeing a Child for Adoption

35

parental rights and duties whereby consent to adoption could
be made final before the adoption application was heard, a
system which is used in various forms in the United States. The
legal problem in systems involving relinquishment is that the
parental rights and duties in respect of a child cannot be left in
a vacuum. This problem is usually overcome by transferring
the parental rights and duties from the natural parent to the
adoption agency on relinquishment. The Committee felt that
such a system should be introduced here whereby the parental
rights and duties in respect of a child could be transferred
from the natural parents to the adoption agency with the
approval of the court. This would enable an adoption agency
to place a child for adoption secure in the knowledge that
consent cannot be withdrawn. Section 14* of the Act
introduces this new system of "freeing a child for adoption"
which enables the question of parental consent to be settled at
an earlier stage than the adoption hearing.

57. Section 14* envisages the procedure of freeing a child for
adoption being used on the application of an adoption agency
in two sets of circumstances. First, where each parent or
guardian of the child freely, and with full understanding of
what is involved, agrees to the making of an adoption order
generally and unconditionally, or secondly where the consent
of the parent or guardian may be dispensed with on one of the
grounds set out in section 12(2)* (discussed later in this
chapter)(section 14(1)*). An application to free a child for
adoption cannot be made by an adoption agency unless it is
made with the consent of each parent or guardian of the child,
or the child is in the care of the agency and the agency is
applying for dispensation of the parental agreement under
section 12(2)* (section 14(2)*). For parental consent to be
effective the child must be at least 6 weeks old (section 14(4)*).
The court cannot dispense with the agreement of any parent or
guardian unless the child is already placed for adoption, or the
court is satisfied that the child is likely to be placed for
adoption (section 14(3)*). Additionally, in Scotland, an order
cannot be made freeing a child for adoption if the child is a
minor (see para. 54) unless the child consents to the order
being made, or the court is satisfied that the minor is
incapable of giving his consent, in which case the court may
dispense with his consent (section 14(5)*).

Procedure on an application to free a child for adoption

58. Whilst an application is pending to free a child for adoption under section 14(1)* a parent or guardian is not entitled to remove the child from the care of the adoption agency except with the leave of the court (section 29* inserting a new section 34* into the 1958 Adoption Act). An application must be made to an "authorised court" which is defined in section 100 of the Act (see para. 82). Such applications will be heard in private in accordance with the provisions of section 21* of the Act (see para. 83). The court may, in accordance with the provisions of section 20* appoint a guardian *ad litem* to safeguard the interests of the child or a reporting officer, a new position created by the Act, for the purposes of witnessing agreements to adoption and ensuring that such agreements are freely given (see para. 85). Every person whose consent to the making of the order is required must be notified of the date and place of the hearing, and of the fact that, unless he wishes or the court requires it, he need not attend (section 22(1)(*b*)*). Parents or guardians who wish to oppose the making of a freeing order will have the right to apply for legal aid (see Schedule 3, para. 82*).

The effects of an order freeing a child for adoption

59. Once an order has been made freeing a child for adoption all the natural parent's rights and duties in respect of the child vest in the adoption agency, as though the adoption agency were adoptive parents (section 14(6)*). The agency then has the right to place the child with prospective adopters and when the adoption application is made the court will have to make its decision on the basis of the welfare of the child and the suitability of the applicants, but not on the question of consent.

Rights of the putative father

60. Although the adoption order can only be granted with the consent of the parents or guardian of a child, unless there are grounds for dispensing with that consent, the father of an

illegitimate child who is not the child's guardian does not count as a parent for this purpose and does not have the right to consent to the child's adoption. All rights in respect of an illegitimate child vest in the child's mother. The putative father does have the right, however, to apply for the custody of the child under section 9 of the Guardianship of Minors Act 1971 and if such an application were made after a child has been freed for adoption, the adoption agency's absolute rights in respect of the child would be contested. To avoid this situation arising section 14(8)* of the Act provides that the court shall not make an order freeing a child for adoption until it is satisfied that, if the child is illegitimate and the putative father is not the guardian of the child, the person claiming to be the father has no intention of applying for custody under section 9 of the Guardianship of Minors Act 1971 (in England and Wales) or under section 2 of the Illegitimate Children (Scotland) Act 1930, or that if he did make such an application it would be unlikely to succeed. This subsection enables the interests of the putative father to be put before the court at the time of the application to free the child for adoption, and once the child has been declared free for adoption his right that once existed under the Guardianship of Minors Act to apply for custody is lost (Schedule 3 to the 1975 Act, para. 75(1)(d)*)

The natural parents' position once a child is freed for adoption

61. When the court makes an order freeing a child for adoption it has a duty to satisfy itself that each parent or guardian who can be found has been given the opportunity, if he so wishes, to make a declaration to the effect that he no longer wishes to be involved in future questions concerning the adoption of the child, and any such declaration must be recorded by the court (section 14(7)*).

62. If a former parent or guardian who was given an opportunity of making a declaration in accordance with section 14(7)* decided not to make such a declaration, he or she is given the right to certain reports about the child by section 15*. The adoption agency is required to inform the former parents within 14 days of the expiry of one year from

the making of the order freeing the child for adoption whether an adoption order has been made or, if not, whether the child has his home with a person with whom he is placed for adoption. There is nothing to prevent an adoption agency informing the former parents at an earlier date than 12 months from the date of the freeing order if an adoption order has been made (section 15(2)*). If an adoption order had not been made at the time of giving notice under the requirements of subsection (2)* the adoption agency has a duty to inform the former parents of any subsequent adoption order and to give the former parent notice whenever the child is placed for adoption or ceases to have his home with a person with whom he was placed for adoption (section 15(3)*).

63. The former parent may give notice to the adoption agency that he prefers not to be involved in future questions concerning the adoption of the child at any time. The agency then has a duty to ensure that such a declaration is recorded by the court that first made the freeing order and the agency is then released from the duty of complying with section 15(3)*, that is, after the first notice is given to the former parent one year from the making of the freeing order, the agency are not required to give any further reports to the former parent.

64. After 12 months have elapsed from the making of the order freeing the child for adoption, the former parent has a right to apply for the revocation of the order on the grounds that he wishes to resume parental rights and duties, provided that an adoption order has not been made in respect of the child or the child has not been placed with prospective adopters (section 16(1)*). While such an application is pending the adoption agency loses the right to place the child for adoption unless it has the leave of the court (section 16(2)*). If the application is granted the parental rights and duties vest in the individual or individuals in whom they vested before the freeing order was made (section 16(3)*). If the parental rights and duties vested in a local authority or voluntary organisation before the freeing order was made, on the granting of an application to revoke a freeing order, the parental rights and duties vest in the person in whom they vested before the local authority or voluntary organisation. This is to ensure that if the court is satisfied that the parent is

justified in asking for the freeing order to be revoked that the local authority's or voluntary organisation's rights in respect of a section 2 resolution (of the Children Act 1948) or of a care order do not automatically revive. Any duty relating to payments which existed towards the child's maintenance before the freeing order revives on the revocation of the order (section 16(3)*).

65. If, however, such an application for revocation is dismissed on the grounds that it would contravene the welfare principle embodied in section 3 (where the child's welfare is the first consideration) then the former parent loses the right to make a further application under section 16(1)* and, moreover, the agency is no longer required to inform the parent of the making of an adoption order, or to inform him that the child has been placed for adoption, or has ceased to have his home with a person with whom he was placed for adoption (section 16(4)*). The court which dismissed the application for revocation may, however, give leave for the former parent to make a further application if it appears to the court to be proper, whether because of change of circumstances or for any other reason (section 16(5)*).

Transfer of parental rights and duties between adoption agencies

66. If an adoption agency has parental rights and duties in respect of a child by virtue of an order made under section 14 and it wishes to transfer these rights and duties to another adoption agency, the adoption agencies may apply jointly to an authorised court which may order such a transfer if it thinks fit (section 23)*. This provision will be especially useful to adoption agencies who have a child in their care who has been freed for adoption with special needs, and another adoption agency has special resources to offer that child.

Which consent procedure to choose

67. The Houghton Committee envisaged that the new procedure of freeing a child for adoption would be one option open to the parent or guardian who preferred to give an early

and final consent to adoption. There will still be parents who would prefer to consent to the making of an adoption order at the time of the adoption application and they will still be able to do this. The new procedure cannot be used in cases which do not involve an adoption agency, that is adoption by relatives or foster parents.

DISPENSING WITH CONSENT

68. The court may be asked to dispense with parental agreement either at the time of the adoption hearing or at the time of an application to free the child for adoption under section 14*. The statutory grounds for dispensing with consent are set out in section 12(2)* of the Act and include the grounds set out in section 5 of the Adoption Act 1958 which is repealed by the new Act. These grounds are that the parent or guardian —

"(a) cannot be found or is incapable of giving his agreement;
 (b) is withholding his consent unreasonably;
 (c) has persistently failed without reasonable cause to discharge the parental duties in relation to the child;
 (d) has abandoned or neglected the child;"

The subsection also includes two new grounds —

"(e) has persistently ill-treated the child;
 (d) has seriously ill-treated the child."

This last ground, section 12(2)(f)*, is subject to the proviso set out in subsection (5)* that, either because of the ill-treatment or for other reasons, the rehabilitation of the child within the household of the parent or guardian is unlikely. The two new grounds extend the powers of local authorities considerably in relation to children who come into care because of ill-treatment and natural parents could find their children being placed for adoption in these circumstances whether they consent to the adoption or not. There are going to be difficulties in establishing proof of whether rehabilitation is likely or not and it is not clear how the courts will interpret this. Resources in local authorities vary enormously and one local authority may be able to rehabilitate a child within his family because of their day-care facilities and home supervision by qualified staff whilst another local authority may be able to offer neither. The new provision punishes natural parents who ill-treat their children in a far more devastating way than any penalty under the criminal law, and it is important that this is borne in mind when deciding to make an application to dispense with consent on this ground.

69. The guiding principle for the court in making decisions as to whether to dispense with consent is embodied in the welfare principle set out in section 3. The court will have to make the long term welfare of the child its first consideration. This will be especially relevant in applications to dispense with consent on the grounds that the parent is withholding his consent unreasonably and may mean that a natural parent who cannot offer the material and educational advantages that the prospective adopters can offer could have his consent dispensed with. In *Re C. (An Infant) 2 All E.R. 478* Diplock L.J. stressed (at p.495) that "...one must look at the whole future of the child; not to mere material affluence in childhood or a better chance through educational advantages to achieve affluence later." The effects of separation on the child from a secure and loving home are factors which may weight strongly with the court but, nevertheless, material wealth and social status will, if other things are equal, be taken into account by the court in assessing what is in the long term interests of the child.

Natural parents' right to legal aid

70. The new Act by amending the Legal Aid Act 1974 gives natural parents the right to apply for legal aid in either adoption proceedings or application to free a child for adoption where one party is opposing the proceedings (Schedule 3, para. 82)* This represents one provision to safeguard the rights of natural parents in an Act which in many ways threatens their rights in respect of their children.

CONSENT SUBJECT TO A CONDITION AS TO RELIGIOUS UPBRINGING

71. The 1958 Act made it possible for natural parents to give

consent to adoption subject to a condition concerning the religious upbringing of the child. The Houghton Committee gave this some consideration and cited as arguments against the retention of this condition three points. First, such a condition is unenforceable as there is no way that the adoptive parents can be made to carry it out once the adoption has gone through. Secondly, such a condition is anomolous as adoption is the complete severance of the legal relationship between the natural parents and the child. Thirdly, if there is a shortage of adopters professing the particular faith named by the mother there is a danger that this might become one of the most important factors governing the selection of suitable prospective adopters, which could be contrary to the child's best interests. The Committee therefore recommended that such a condition should no longer be allowed. The Bill did not include the right for natural parents to make a condition concerning the religious upbringing of the child, but in the House of Lords many of their Lordships regretted this. The Act itself now repeals the provision in the 1958 Act whereby parents could give consent to adoption subject to a condition concerning religious upbringing and includes a requirement that adoption agencies shall, so far as is practicable, have regard when placing a child for adoption to any wishes of the natural parents regarding the religious upbringing of the child (section 13). This seems to represent a neat compromise between the two views on the subject.

Adoption Procedure

This chapter looks at the procedure leading up to the making of an adoption order, and at what happens if a full adoption order is refused.

THE APPLICATION FOR AN ADOPTION ORDER

In Cases where an Adoption Agency is Involved

72. Where a child has been placed with prospective adopters by an adoption agency the child must have lived with the applicants at all times during the 13 weeks preceding the adoption hearing. The first six weeks of an infant's life do not count in this period of 13 weeks so that the child must be at least 19 weeks old before the adoption order can be made (section 9(1)*).

73. The local authority is no longer required to perform "welfare supervision" in respect of a child placed for adoption by an adoption agency as it had to under the 1958 Act. The worker from the adoption agency who arranged the placement of the child will have the responsibility of helping the prospective adopters with any problems they have related to the settling in of the child. The adoption order can only be granted if the court is satisfied that sufficient opportunities to see the child with the applicant or the applicants, as the case may be, in their home environment have been afforded to the adoption agency (section 9(3)*). The adoption agency is required to submit a report to the court on the suitability of the applicants and any other matters relevant to the operation of section 3 (this includes ensuring that first consideration is being given to the need to safeguard and promote the welfare of the child throughout his childhood, and also to ascertain the

child's feelings about the adoption if he is old enough) and the agency has a general duty to assist the court in any matter that the court may direct (section 22(3)*). The agency's role in this is very similar to the role of the guardian *ad litem* in the 1958 Act procedure.

In Cases where an Adoption Agency is not Involved

74. Where the applicant or one of the applicants is a parent, step-parent or relative of the child, the child must have had his home with the applicants or one of them for a period of at least 13 weeks preceding the making of the adoption order, not including the first 6 weeks of the child's life (section 9(1)(a)*). Where the applicant(s) are not relatives and where the child has not been placed for adoption by an adoption agency, the child must be at least 12 months old and have had his home with the applicant(s) or one of them for at least 12 months preceding the making of the order (section 9(2)*). As section 28* prohibits third party placements (see para. 51) the circumstances in which this requirement operates must be relatively rare. It would apply to children who were placed by third parties prior to the Act coming into force, or to children who had been fostered by applicants who subsequently decided to adopt.

75. In both these cases the applicant is required to give the local authority within whose area he has his home at least three months' notice of his intention to apply for an adoption order (section 18(1)*). The adoption order can only be granted if the court is satisfied that sufficient opportunities to see the child with the applicant or applicants, as the case may be, in the home environment have been afforded to that local authority (section 9(3)*). Once the local authority have received notice in accordance with section 18* they have a duty to investigate the matter and submit a report to the court. They have a duty to investigate the suitability of the applicants and any other matters relevant to the operation of section 3. The authority also has a duty to report to the court whether the child was placed with the applicants in contravention of the new provision (section 28*) prohibiting third party placements (section 18(3)(b)*). Thus in adoption applications where an

agency is not involved the local authority has a role incorporating elements of their role in welfare supervision and of their role under the 1958 Act as guardian *ad litem*.

Restrictions on removing a child pending adoption

76. Security for the child whilst an adoption application is pending is ensured by certain restrictions which are placed on the removal of the child from prospective adopters during this time. Section 29* of the Act replaces and extends section 34 of the 1958 Act. This section covers two situations. First, where an adoption application is pending where the parents or guardian of the child have agreed to the making of an adoption order (whether or not they knew the identity of the applicant), the parent or guardian is not entitled to remove the child from the custody of the person with whom the child has his home against that person's will except with the leave of the court (the new section 34(1)*). Secondly, where an application for an order freeing a child for adoption is pending and the child is in the care of an adoption agency and the application was made with the consent of each parent or guardian, then again no parent or guardian is entitled to remove the child from the custody of the person with whom the child has his home against that person's will except with the leave of the court (the new section 34(2)*). A person who contravenes either of these provision is liable on conviction to three months' imprisonment or a fine not exceeding £400 or both (the new section 34(3)*).

77. Section 29* also enacts a new section 34A* to be inserted into the 1958 Act. This places restrictions on the removal of the child where the applicant has provided a home for the child for five years or more. No one is entitled to remove the child in these circumstances while an adoption application is pending against the will of the applicants except with the leave of the court or by authority conferred by any enactment (such as a place of safety order made in accordance with the provisions of the Children and Young Persons Act 1969), or on the arrest of the child. Section 34A* further provides that where a local authority is given notice under section 18* of the 1975 Act that a person intends to apply for an adoption order

in respect of a child who has had his home with the prospective adopters for the previous five years, no one is entitled to remove the child except with the leave of the court or under authority conferred by any enactment or on the arrest of the child before either the prospective adopters apply for an adoption order or the expiry of the period of three months' notice whichever occurs first (section 34A(2)*). Thus foster parents who have cared for a child for five years or more are protected, in most circumstances, from the time they give notice to the local authority of their intention to adopt up until the time of the hearing, from having the child removed by the natural parents, by the local authority or by anyone else. If however the foster parents give notice of their intention to adopt and three months later have not applied for a hearing, then the period of protection comes to an end. They may subsequently decide to adopt again and again give notice to the local authority of their intention to adopt but they will only have the protection of section 34A(2)* if that notice is given at least 28 days after the expiry of three months from the original notice (section 34A(5)*). As in section 34* a person who contravenes this section will be liable on conviction to a fine not exceeding £400 or three months' imprisonment or both (section 34A(6)*). If the local authority receives notice from prospective adopters in these circumstances in respect of a child whom the authority knows to be in the care of another local authority or voluntary organisation they have a duty to inform that authority or organisation within 7 days from the receipt of the notice (section 34A(4)*).

78. It is made clear by subsection (3)* that these provisions apply where a child was in the care of the local authority at the time when he first began to have his home with the applicants, or where the child continues to be in the care of a local authority at the time of the application. In neither case does the local authority have the right to remove the child except with the written consent of the foster parents with the leave of the court, or on the refusal of the application by the court. In both these cases the foster parents have 7 days in which to return the child. The local authority may forgo the right to have the child returned, if the child was in care at the time of the notice of intention to adopt. These exceptions are set out in

sections 35 and 36 of the Adoption Act 1959. In Scotland, subsection (3)* does not apply where the removal of the child has been authorised by a place of safety order made by a justice of the peace or a children's hearing in accordance with Part III of the Social Work (Scotland) Act 1968 (subs.(8)*).

79. Section 34A* is designed to protect the interests of foster parents who decide to adopt and also to safeguard the interests of children, who would in most cases suffer if they were removed precipitantly from the foster parents with whom they have had their home for at least five years. It does not give the foster parents any additional rights at the adoption hearing where the application will be dealt with on its merits. As such it does not represent a serious infringement of natural parents' rights, although this section has been opposed on this ground. The time limit of five years specified in section 34A* may be varied by the Secretary of State by a statutory instrument in the light of how this provision works out in practice. This is the first section in the Act in which time limits are mentioned but they are used in other sections of the Act. There has been some controversy over the use of time limits, many people being completely against the idea (the British Association of Social Workers for example has opposed the idea of time limits) whereas others have criticised time limits for being insufficiently sensitive to the needs of the individual child. Five years for a young child can be a lifetime whilst a teenager would not regard it as being so long. The Association of British Adoption Agencies agree with the idea of time limits as they emphasise the importance of the passage of time in a child's life and the need to make decisions in relation to the child, and they may enable a more effective protection of the rights of the child. In the case of this particular time limit when the Act was still at its Committee stage in the House of Lords there was a move to lower the five year limit to two years on the grounds that five years is an inordinately long time in the life of a child, especially a very young child. The amendment to two years was rejected on the grounds that the Act itself enabled the time limit to be varied in practice and the right balance should be found in this way.

Return of a child taken away in breach of sections
34* and 34A* of 1958 Act

80. If a child has been removed from the custody of a person
in breach of sections 34* or 34A* of the 1958 Act, an
authorised court may, on the application of that person order
that the child should be returned to him (section 30(1)*). If a
person has "reasonable grounds" for believing that another
person is intending to remove a child from the applicant's
custody in breach of sections 34* or 34A* he may apply to an
authorised court to order that the other person does not
remove the child (section 30(2)*). If an order is made under
subsection (1)* by the High Court and the High Court is
satisfied that the child has not been returned to the applicant,
the court may order an officer of the court to search the
premises which are specified in the order for the return of the
child, and if the officer finds the child to return the child to
the applicant. This provision similarly applies to an order
made in the country court (subs.(3)*). If a justice of the peace
is satisfied by information given on oath that there are
"reasonable grounds" for believing that a child, to whom an
order under subsection (1)* relates, is in premises specified in
the information, he may issue a search warrant authorising a
constable to search premises for the child. If a constable acting
in pursuance of this warrant finds the child he is to return the
child to the person who applied for the order (subs.(4)*). The
provisions contained in subsections (3)* and (4)* do not apply
to Scotland. An authorised court for this purpose is defined in
section 100(7) as, if there is an application for an adoption
order or an order freeing a child for adoption pending, the
court in which that order is pending, or in any other case, the
High Court, the county court within whose district the
applicant lives or the magistrates' court within whose area the
applicant lives.

THE HEARING

Notice of the hearing

81. Unless a child has already been freed for adoption, every
person whose agreement to the making of an adoption order or

an order freeing the child for adoption is required to be given or dispensed with under this Act must be notified of the date and place of the hearing, if he or she can be found (section 22(1)*). The person must also be told that unless he wishes to attend or the court requires him to attend his attendance at the adoption hearing is not compulsory (section 22(1)*).

The court

82. The Adoption Act 1958, section 9(1) and the Adoption Court Rules empower adoption applications to be made to the Family Division of the High Court (this happens very rarely), or to the county court or the magistrates' court within whose jurisdiction the applicant or the infant resides at the date of the application. The Houghton Committee when considering the courts involved in adoption applications felt that a unified system of family courts would have advantages over this tripartite division of jurisdiction. They made no recommendation in this respect as the whole subject of family courts was being examined by the Law Commission at that time. The Act does not change the courts which may deal with adoption applications at this stage, with the exception that in the magistrates' court applications will no longer be heard by the juvenile court but by the magistrates' court sitting as for domestic proceedings, as they do when hearing applications for an order under the Guardianship Acts or separation orders (see para. 28). Section 100 sets out the definition of 'authorised court" in the new Act and replaces section 9(1) of the 1958 Act. In relation to England and Wales an authorised court is —

"(a) the High Court;
(b) the county court within whose district the child is and, in the case of an application under section 14 any county court within whose district a parent or guardian of the child is;
(c) any other county court prescribed by rules made under section 102 of the County Courts Act 1959;
(d) a magistrates' court within whose area the child is and, in the case of an application under section 14, a magistrates' court within whose area a parent or guardian of the child is."

If the child is in Scotland when the application is made the following are authorised courts —
"(*a*) the Court of Session;
  (*b*) the sheriff court of the sheriffdom within which the child is."
Thus, with the exception of applications to free a child for adoption under section 14*, where the child is, rather than where the applicants are is the deciding factor in determining to which court the application should be made. If the child is not in Great Britain at the time of the application for an adoption order, or an order freeing a child for adoption, then the application must be made to the High Court (for England and Wales) or the Court of Session (for Scotland)(section 100(4)). The definition of "authorised court" could change in the future if the Government goes ahead with its commitment to introduce a system of family courts.

Hearings of applications in private

83. In practice all adoption applications are heard in private although section 9(2) of the 1958 Act (repealed by the 1975 Act) merely states that "Adoption Rules may provide for applications for adoption orders being heard and determined otherwise than in open court...." Section 21* of the 1975 Act states that in the High Court all applications may be heard in chambers, in the county court all proceedings must be heard and determined *in camera*, and in the magistrates' court the proceedings shall be domestic proceedings (which are always heard in private) with no journalist or reporters permitted to be present. In Scotland all proceedings should be heard and determined *in camera* unless the court otherwise directs. This section ensures that proceedings should be in private, both in the case of adoption applications and of applications to free a child for adoption.

Role of the guardian ad litem and reporting officer

84. Under the 1958 Act procedure in adoption applications the placing agency and the local authority did not report directly to the court, but this was done by the guardian *ad*

litem who was appointed in all adoption applications. The duty of the guardian *ad litem* was to safeguard the interests of the child before the court in the first place, and to investigate and report on all the circumstances relevant to the adoption application. He also had the duty to ensure that all consents were freely given and of verifying statements contained in the application. The Houghton Committee considered the role of the guardian *ad litem* and felt that the court ought to have a first hand account of the judgments and assessments made by the adoption agency, and that the agency should have a duty to prepare a report for the court on the suitability of the applicants. This would avoid two social workers, one from the agency and one from the local authority carrying out the duties of the guardian *ad litem*, needing to be involved with the prospective adopters and duplicating their enquiries. As we have seen this recommendation is given effect by section 22(3)* of the new Act where in agency cases the adoption agency has to prepare a report for the court. In non-agency cases the local authority has a duty to submit a report to the court on the suitability of the applicants in accordance with section 18(2)* of the new Act.

85. The Houghton Committee recommended that the role of the guardian *ad litem* should not be mandatory but that the court should have a discretionary power to appoint a guardian *ad litem* in certain situations, for example where certain aspects of an adoption application need investigating. The Committee also recommended that there should be another person involved in adoption proceedings called a reporting officer who would witness agreements to adoptions and have a duty to report on whether the parents had freely given their consent after having considered the alternatives. The new Act gives effect to these recommendations in section 20*. This provides that rules shall provide for the appointment of a guardian *ad litem* in such cases as the rules may prescribe in adoption hearings and also in applications to free a child for adoption. Section 20* also provides for the appointment of a reporting officer in such hearings, again in such cases as the rules may prescribe. The duty of the guardian *ad litem* will be "to safeguard the interests of the child in the prescribed manner." The role of the reporting officer is to witness

agreements to adoptions and performing such other duties as
the rules may prescribe. Guardians *ad litem* and reporting
officers are required to be appointed independently of the
adoption agency who placed the child, or made the
application to free the child for adoption, or held the parental
rights and duties relating to the child where there is an
application to revoke a freeing order. However, a guardian *ad
litem* and reporting officer may be appointed from the staff of
the same local authority which is preparing a report for the
court in a non-agency adoption application. A guardian *ad
litem* and reporting officer may be the same person if the court
thinks fit (section 20(2)*). The Secretary of State will make
provision for the establishment of a panel of persons who may
be appointed as guardians *ad litem* or reporting officers in
accordance with rules which have yet to be drafted (section
103(1)). It seems likely that this panel will consist not only of
local authority social workers and probation officers but also of
others, perhaps retired persons, who have experience in this
field.

WHERE THE COURT DOES NOT MAKE A FINAL ORDER

If the court is not satisfied with all the circumstances
surrounding an application it may refuse to make a final
order.

Where an adoption order is refused

86. Under the provisions of the 1958 Act (section 35(3))
where the court refuses an application for an adoption order or
the application is withdrawn in respect of a child placed by an
adoption agency, the child must be returned to the agency
within seven days of the notice of refusal or withdrawal. The
Houghton Committee felt that this period was too short and
did not enable the agency to make plans to introduce the child
to a new home. They recommended that the court should have
discretion to extend this seven-day period to a maximum of six
weeks from the refusal or withdrawal of the order. This would
give the agency time to plan the gradual introduction of the
child into a new home and would also give the applicants time

to consider lodging an appeal where appropriate. Section 31*
of the new Act inserts a new subsection into section 35 of the
1958 Act to this effect. The court on refusing an adoption
order is given discretion to extend the period of seven days
during which the child must be returned to the agency to a
period not exceeding six weeks and this period must be
specified in the order.

87. Where the court refuses to make an order in a case
where an adoption agency was not involved the Houghton
Committee recommended that the court should have power to
make an alternative order, such as a supervision order or care
order. Section 17* of the Act enacts this recommendation, and
provides that, in relation to a child under 16, the court may on
refusing to make an adoption order make a supervision order
to the local authority or to a probation officer where
exceptional circumstances make this desirable, or to make a
care order where it is impracticable or undesirable for the
child to be entrusted to the parents or to any other individual.
The conditions relating to supervision orders and care orders
made under the Guardianship of Minors Acts 1971 and 1973
relate to orders made under this section. These provisions
relate both to England and Wales and to Scotland (see para.
121).

Interim orders

88. The court has power under section 8 of the 1958 Act to
defer making a full adoption order and to make an interim
order giving the custody of the child to the applicants for a
probationary period not exceeding two years. The Houghton
Committee wondered if this provision was strictly necessary but
concluded that it should be retained. Section 19* of the Act
re-enacts the power of the court to make interim orders and
section 8 of the 1958 Act is repealed. The new section gives the
court the power to make an order vesting the legal custody of
the child in the prospective adopters for a period not exceeding
two years and to postpone determining the adoption
application provided that the child is either free for adoption
or the parents have consented freely to the application or their
agreement may be dispensed with on one of the grounds set out

in section 12(2)*, and that the local authority has been given three months' notice of the application in accordance with section 18(1)*, if applicable. If a court decides to make such an order it may make terms for the maintenance of the child and such other conditions as it thinks fit. If the court specifies a probationary period of less than two years in an interim order it may extend the order to a period not exceeding two years in aggregate by a further order.

7 Convention Adoption Orders and Proposed Foreign Adoptions

This chapter looks at the provisions of the 1975 Act, first in relation to Convention adoption orders and secondly in relation to proposed foreign adoptions.

CONVENTION ADOPTION ORDERS

89. The Hague Convention on Adoption in 1965, to which the United Kingdom was a signatory, sought to make adoptions possible between different countries and to overcome problems where the applicant resides in a different country to the child. The 1968 Adoption Act enacted the terms of the Hague Convention but this Act has not yet been brought into force and the Convention has not as yet been ratified by the United Kingdom. It is expected that the Convention will eventually be ratified by the United Kingdom and this is brought a step nearer by certain amendments to the 1968 Act which are made by the 1975 Act.

90. As we have seen in Chapter 4 an application for an adoption order is dependent on the applicant, or in the case of a married couple, at least one of them, being domiciled in a part of the United Kingdom, or in the Channel Islands or the Isle of Man, or the application must be for a Convention adoption order and the provisions of section 24* must be complied with. Not all countries use our concept of domicile to define their jurisdiction and to overcome this, jurisdiction is based on the concepts of nationality and habitual residence in the case of Convention adoption orders.

Section 24* of the Act sets out certain conditions in relation to the child and in relation to the applicants which have to be satisfied both at the time of the application and at the time of the making of the order if a Convention adoption order is to be made.

Conditions in relation to the child

91. The child must be a national of the United Kingdom or a national of a Convention country and must habitually reside in British territory or a Convention country, and must not be, or have been, married (section 24(2)*). A Convention country is defined in section 107 of the Act as a country outside British territory which is for the time being designated by an order of the Secretary of State as a country in which, in his opinion, the Convention is in force. The definition of habitual residence is left by the Hague Convention for each country to define for itself. The concept seems to mean a person's usual dwelling-place where he is accustomed to living, and implies residence over a period of time.

Conditions in relation to the applicants

(i) In the case of an application by a married couple

92. In the case of an application by a married couple either
"(*a*) each must be a United Kingdom national or a national of a Convention country, and both must habitually reside in Great Britain, or
(*b*) both must be United Kingdom nationals, and each must habitually reside in British territory or a Convention country." (subs.(4)*)
If both the applicants are nationals of the same Convention country the adoption must not be prohibited by a "specified provision" of the internal law of that country. "Specified provision" is defined in subsection (8)* as "a provision specified in an order of the Secretary of State as one notified to the Government of the United Kingdom in pursuance of the provisions of the Convention which relate to prohibitions on an adoption contained in the national law of the Convention country in question."

(ii) In the case of an application by a single person

93. In the case of an application by a single person either —
"(*a*) he must be a United Kingdom national or a national of a Convention country, and must habitually reside in

Great Britain, or
   (*b*) he must be a United Kingdom nationa, and must habitually reside in British territory or a Convention country." (subs.(5)*)

If he is a national of a Convention country the adoption must not be prohibited by a "specified provision" of the internal law of the country (as defined above).

94. A Convention adoption order cannot be made if the applicant or applicants and the child are all nationals of the United Kingdom living in British territory (s.24(3)*.

The consent procedure

95. If the child is not a national of the United Kingdom the order can only be granted if consents to the making of the order have been made in accordance with the internal law of the Convention country of which the child is a national. The court must also be satisfied that each person who consents to the order in accordance with that internal law does so with the full understanding of what is involved (section 24(6)*). The term "consents and consultations" which subsection (6)* uses does not include the consent of and consultation with the applicant and members of the applicant's family. Consents will be proved in the manner prescribed by the rules. The courts will have power to dispense with consent under the internal law mentioned in subsection (6)*.

96. Where the provisions of the internal law of the Convention country of which the child is a national require the attendance before the court of a person who does not reside in Great Britain that requirement will be treated as satisfied if that person has been given a reasonable opportunity of communicating his opinion on the adoption to the appropriate officer or clerk of the court, or to an appropriate authority of the country in question for transmission to the court, and where he has availed himself of that opportunity, his opinion has been transmitted to the court.

Courts which may make Convention adoption orders

97. In England and Wales only the High Court may make a

Convention adoption order. In Scotland this power is restricted to the Court of Session (section 100(5)).

Notification of the hearing

98. In the case of an application for a Convention adoption order, rules shall require that every person who can be found and whose agreement to the making of the order would be required if the application were for an adoption order to be notified of the date and the place of the hearing, and of the fact that unless he wishes to attend or the court requires it, he need not attend (section 22(2)*).

PROPOSED FOREIGN ADOPTIONS

99. If a person who is not domiciled (for the definition of domicile see para. 45) in this country wishes to adopt a child under the law of the country in which he is domiciled, he may apply to an authorised court here for an order vesting the parental rights and duties in him (section 25*). This provision is to help a small but important minority of children who may be better placed with parents of their own ethnic group. The domicile requirements would prevent a full adoption order being made here. Most of the provisions set out in the Act relating to adoption applications apply also to these applications (section 25(2)*). There is an additional requirement however that a child must be at least 32 weeks old and have been with the applicants or one of them for the 26 weeks preceding the application. An authorised court for the purpose of an application under this section is either the High Court or the county court in England and Wales, and the Court of Sessions or the sheriff court in Scotland (section 100(6)). **Entries in the Register of Births shall be** marked "Proposed Foreign Adoption" or "Proposed Foreign Re-adoption" as the case may be (section 25(3)*). This section replaces section 53 of the 1958 Act which is repealed by the new Act.

Custodianship

100. The new status of custodianship which the Act introduces has its origins in a recommendation of the Houghton Committee. The Committee felt that there should be a legal status, falling short of adoption, which gave relatives caring for a child and foster parents looking after a child in long term care legal security in their relationship with the child. They considered in particular the ever-growing proportion of adopters who were relatives or step-parents of the child who seemed to be using adoption, perhaps because of the lack of an appropriate alternative, to give their relationship with the child legal security. The Committee felt that such adoptions had certain disadvantages and were not always in the child's best interests.

101. Adoptions by relatives fall into three broad categories. The largest category is adoption by parent and step-parent, which includes both adoption of children of a previous marriage and of illegitimate children. Adoption in these circumstances enables the step-parent to assume jointly with their spouse the parental rights and duties in relation to the child. The child, on his adoption, receives a new birth certificate, becomes a member of the new family in a legal sense and, in the case of adoption by mother and step-father, will take the step-father's surname. But such adoptions sever the child's relationship with the other half of his natural family and if used to disguise from the child the reality of his family background could be harmful. The second category is adoption by a single person of their own child, most usually adoption by a single woman. Adoption does not confer upon the single mother any additional rights but does sever any

rights that the putative father might have, such as the right to apply for custody under the Guardianship of Minors Act 1971. Again if the adoption is an attempt to hide from the child the fact that he is illegitimate it may not be in his best interests. The third category is adoption by relatives other than parents. Adoption is used by relatives when caring for a child to give their relationship legal security but has the disadvantage of distorting inter-family relationships. Adoption severs the existing blood relationships within the family, in law, although it cannot do so in fact. Thus a child adopted by his grandparents finds they are now his parents and his mother becomes his sister. Such tortuous relationships are at best confusing for the child if he is aware of them but are also potentially very damaging should he only discover the adoption later on in life.

102. The Houghton Committee recommended that as a general rule adoptions by relatives should be replaced by a new legal status which did not involve the complete severance of links with other members of the child's natural family. But they felt there might be exceptional circumstances which would justify adoptions by relatives and did not therefore recommend that they should be absolutely prohibited. The Committee also felt that this new status would be of use to foster parents who do not wish to adopt but who do want to have greater security in their relationship with the child. Their recommendation was that the right to apply for custody of a child, which in England and Wales only extends to parents, should be extended to relatives and in some circumstances to foster parents already caring for a child. A custody order vests all the parental rights and duties in respect of a child in the person to whom the order is granted but, unlike adoption, does not sever the child's links with his natural family and is not irrevocable. The Committee called this new right to apply for custody "guardianship." The idea of relatives and foster parents being able to apply for custody is introduced in the new Act but is called "custodianship," a somewhat clumsy word, which seems to have been chosen in preference to guardianship to avoid confusion with the existing status of guardianship.

CUSTODIANSHIP — WHAT RIGHTS DOES IT CONFER?

103. The provisions relating to custodianship are set out in Part II* of the Act. Section 33* provides that a person who is not the mother or father of the child may, in certain circumstances apply to the court for an order to vest the legal custody of the child in them. This order is to be called a custodianship order and a person to whom such an order is granted, the custodian. Prior to this a person who was not a parent (and for this purpose parent includes a putative father) did not have the right to apply for custody. The only means by which someone who was not a parent could obtain legal security in their relationship with a child they were caring for, in England and Wales, was to make the child a ward of court and to ask the court to appoint them as guardian. In Scotland this right existed before the Act and sections 47* to 55* extend and clarify the existing common law rights for persons other than parents who apply for custody.

104. In section 33* a custodianship order is defined as an "order vesting the legal custody of a child in the applicant." The term "legal custody" is explained in section 86. This section provides that legal custody means in this Act —

> "so much of the parental rights and duties as relate to the person of the child (including the place and manner in which his time is spent); but a person shall not by virtue of having legal custody of a child be entitled to effect or arrange for his emigration from the United Kingdom unless he is a parent or guardian of the child."

Thus a custodianship order confers upon the custodian the right to make day to day decisions concerning the child. He would be able to consent to a child's marriage, or make arrangements for the child's education or consent to the administration of an anaesthetic to a child who had to undergo surgery. But it does not give the custodian the right to arrange for a child's emigration or to consent to his adoption. He will not have the right to change a child's name, neither will he receive a new birth certificate in respect of the child as he would have done on adoption.

105. One of the major differences from adoption is that a custodianship order may be revoked on the application of the

parents or guardian, a local authority, or the custodian himself. The custodianship order carries with it rights to maintenance and to access. Where the order is made in respect of an illegitimate child and an order has not been made previously under the Affiliation Proceedings Act 1957, the custodian has the right to apply for an affiliation order provided that he does so within three years of being granted the custodianship order (section 45)*. The custodian has the right to "actual custody" of the child and this may be enforced against any other person who unlawfully assumes actual custody of the child. Actual custody is defined in the Act in section 87:

> "A person has actual custody of a child if he has actual possession of his person, whether or not that possession is shared with one or more other persons."

WHO MAY APPLY FOR A CUSTODIANSHIP ORDER

106. Section 33(3)* of the Act outlines the persons who are qualified to apply for a custodianship order. Three general sets of circumstances are set out in that subsection in which persons are qualified to apply. Subsections (4)*(5)* and (8)* place restrictions on certain categories of relatives and step-parents who might have qualified under the three general heads and subsection (3)* has to be read in the light of these restrictions.

107. The three general sets of circumstances in which persons are qualified to apply are first —

> "(a) a relative or step-parent of the child —
>
> > (*i*) who applies with the consent of the person having legal custody of the child, and
> >
> > (*ii*) with whom the child has had his home for the three months preceding the making of the application;"

A "relative" is defined in section 107 as having the same meaning as in the 1958 Act. In that Act relatives of the child are defined as a "grandparent, brother, sister, uncle or aunt, whether of the full or half blood or by affinity" and includes the natural father of an illegitimate child. Section 87(3) clarifies the phrase "person with whom a child has his home." This subsection provides that:

> "In this Act, unless the context otherwise requires,

references to the person with whom a child has his home refer to the person who, disregarding absence of the child at a hospital or boarding school and any other temporary absence, has actual custody of the child."

Thus in section 33(3)(*a*)* as long as the applicant has actual custody of the child, the three month period will run from the time he acquired actual custody and periods spent away from home or at boarding school do not prevent the three month period from running from that time.

Secondly, any person is qualified to apply for a custodianship order,

"(*i*) who applies with the consent of the person having legal custody of the child, and

(*ii*) with whom the child has had his home for a period or periods before the making of the application which amount to at least twelve months and include the three months preceding the making of the application;"

Thirdly, "any person with whom the child has had his home for a period or periods before the making of the application which amount to at least three years and include the three months preceding the making of the application."

It is only under this third general head that it is possible to apply for a custodianship order without the consent of the person having legal custody. But the requirement under the first two heads that the person having legal custody must consent to the application may be dispensed with if no one has legal custody of the applicant himself has legal custody or the person having legal custody cannot be found (subs.(6)*).

108. The mother or father of the child cannot be eligible in any circumstances to apply for custodianship (section 33(4)*). A step-parent is not qualified to apply either if the child was named in any order as to custody following proceedings for divorce or nullity of marriage. In these circumstances a variation of custody order would have to be sought in the divorce court instead (section 33(5)*). This last subsection does not apply however if the parent other than the one the step-parent married cannot be found or if an order was made as to custody in the divorce court in respect of the child whom it was later found was not a "child of the family." "Child of the family" means in this case a child of both the parties or any

other child, excluding a child who has been boarded out with
the parties by a local authority or a voluntary organisation,
who has been treated by both of the parties as a child of the
family.

109. The provisions of section 33* do not apply to Scotland
as the right of persons other than parents to apply for custody
already exists there. Neither do the provisions of section 34* to
46* apply to Scotland. Sections 47* to 55* clarify the existing
provisions in Scotland in relation to custody and in some cases
extend these. The term custodianship is not used in relation to
proceedings in Scotland, where the term custody is used in all
cases. Section 47(2)* sets out broadly similar qualifications as
to who may apply for custody as those set out in section 33* in
relation to England and Wales. In Scotland however the
qualifications imposed on applicants in relation to the period
of care and possession of the child and in relation to the
consent of the parents may be disregarded if the applicant can
show cause why an order should be made awarding him the
custody of the child (section 47(2)(*d*)*). In relation to
Scotland, a child is defined as a person under 16.

EFFECTS OF THE ORDER ON EXISTING CUSTODY

110. A custodianship order has the effect of suspending the
rights of any person other than the custodian to the legal
custody of the child, except where the person having custody is
a parent of the child and the person who becomes the
custodian is the husband or wife of that parent. In this
situation both the husband and wife have the legal custody
jointly (section 44(2)*). If a custodianship order is revoked
then the rights of the person who had legal custody before the
order was made are revived. This would apply equally to
situations where the parents previously had custody or a local
authority had parental rights, for example, under section 2 of
the Children Act 1948.

9 Custodianship Procedure

The procedure leading up to the application for and the granting of a custodianship order is examined in this chapter as well as the procedure for variation and revocation of such orders. The chapter concludes with a discussion on the effectiveness of custodianship as an alternative to adoption.

THE GUIDING PRINCIPLE FOR THE COURT IN DETERMINING DISPUTES OVER CUSTODY

111. In Part I of the Act the guiding principle for the court in adoption proceedings is that first consideration should be given to the need to safeguard and promote the welfare of the child throughout his childhood. In Part II* however which deals with applications for custody there is a different guiding principle for the court. Here, as in all custody proceedings, the welfare of the child is to be the first and paramount consideration. This is not explicitly stated in the Act but section 33(9)* makes it clear that the principle enacted in section 1 of the Guardianship of Minors Act 1971 applies to applications for a custodianship order. Section 1 of the Act provides:

"Where in any proceedings before any court (whether or not a court as defined in section 15 of this Act) —
  (*a*) the custody or upbringing of a minor; or
  (*b*) the administration of any property belonging to or held on trust for a minor or the application of the income thereof,
is in question, the court in deciding that question shall regard the welfare of the minor as the first and paramount consideration, and shall not take into consideration whether from any other oint of view the claim of the father, in respect of such custody, upbringing administration or

application is superior to that of the mother, or the claim of the mother is superior to that of the father."

112. Thus in custodianship proceedings the court will have to weigh all the circumstances that are of any relevance to the case but in reaching a decision the court must give first and paramount consideration to the interests of the child. This is the welfare test which the court has to apply in all custody proceedings. The "paramountcy" test gives even greater weight to the interests of the child than the "first consideration" test and thus the court's decision-making has a different emphasis in contested custody applications from that in contested adoption applications. But it is clear that this test is not an objective formula and each case has to be decided on its individual merits. What are seen as the interests of the child depend very much on the prevailing climate of sociological and psychological thought and on how far the judges deciding the case have absorbed this. Thus at present there is a swing of opinion away from the rights of natural parents towards the rights of children and the duties of parents, and the natural parent is no longer necessarily regarded as the best person to bring up the child. Twenty years ago this would not have been so. In a contested application for a custodianship order between foster parents and natural parents, the foster parents would not necessarily have to show that the natural parents were unfit in some way, as a local authority has to in a resolution under section 2 of the Children Act 1948 or in care proceedings, but would have to prove that it was in the child's interests to remain with them. As in a contested application the child would have had to have had his home with them for at least three years and by this time evidence could probably be adduced to show that it would be harmful to separate the child from its foster parents who had cared for the child for at least three years, particularly in the case of a younger child, the natural parents stand at a severe disadvantage in such applications.

NOTICE OF APPLICATION TO BE GIVEN TO THE LOCAL AUTHORITY

113. The applicant for a custodianship order must give

notice of the application to the local authority within whose area the child resides within seven days or such extended period as the court of the local authority allow (section 40(1)* in relation to England and Wales). The provisions in relation to Scotland are different in that where a relative, step-parent or foster parent of the child applies for a custody order and resides in Scotland at the time of the application he must give notice to the local authority within whose area he resides (rather than where the child resides) within seven days of the application (section 49(1)*).

PREPARATION OF A REPORT BY THE LOCAL AUTHORITY

114. In England and Wales once a local authority has received notice of an application for a custodianship order they have a duty to arrange for an officer of the authority to prepare a report on matters relevant to the application (section 40(2)*). The Secretary of State is to prescribe in regulations the matters which this report must cover, but they include the means and suitability of the applicant, the means of the mother and father of the child and their wishes regarding the application, and the wishes and feelings of the child having regard to his age and understanding and "all other matters relevant to the operation of section 1 ... of the Guardianship of Minors Act 1971 in relation to the application." The matters referred to in section 1 of that Act are "the custody or upbringing of a minor; and the administration of any property belonging to or held on trust for a minor, and the application of the income thereof." The report must also include such information relating to the members of the applicant's household as the regulations prescribe. These requirements are set out in subsection (3)*. A report which is submitted to a magistrates' court under this section is governed by the provisions of subsections (2), (3) and (3A) of section 6 of the Guardianship Act 1973 which are amended by section 90 of the 1975 Act. The report may be given either orally or in writing. If in writing a copy of the report must be given to each party to the proceedings or his counsel or solicitor either before or during the hearing. If the court thinks fit it may

order the report or any part of it to be read aloud during the hearing. The court may, and if requested to do so by a party to the proceedings or by his counsel or solicitor, shall require the officer who prepared the report to give evidence on matters referred to in the report and if the officer gives evidence, any party to the proceedings may call evidence with respect to any matter referred to by the officer. The court may take account of the report and of any evidence given by the officer on his report "notwithstanding any enactment or rule of law to the contrary." (section 90 amending section 6 of the Guardianship Act 1973).

115. In addition to the duty which the local authority has under section 40* to prepare a report for the court once it has been notified of an application for a custodianship order, the court also has the power to request a report from the local authority or from a probation officer with respect to any "specified matter which appears to the court to be relevant to the application" either orally or in writing (section 39)*. Again the provisions of the Guardianship Act 1973, section 6(2) to (6) as amended by section 90 of the 1975 Act apply to reports requested under this section. This power to request reports is given in any hearing relating to custodianship proceedings so that a report may be requested on applications to vary or revoke an order, on applications for access and maintenance under section 34*, where there is a dispute between joint custodians or in cases where the court decides to treat an application for an adoption order or a guardianship order as an application for a custodianship order (section 37*).

116. In Scotland the local authority is required by section 49* to investigate and report to the court on all the circumstances of the child and on the proposed arrangements for the care and upbringing of the child when they receive notice of an application for custody by a relative, step-parent or foster parent of the child. Section 12(2) of the Guardianship Act, paragraphs (*b*) and (*c*) are deemed to apply to this report (section 49(3)*). These paragraphs provide:

"(*b*) If on consideration of a report furnished in pursuance of this subsection the court, either *ex proprio motu* [of its own accord] or on the application of any person concerned, thinks it expedient to do so, it may require the person who furnished the report to appear and be examined on oath regarding any matter dealt with in the report, and such person may be examined or cross-examined accordingly.

(*c*) Any expenses incurred in connection with the preparation of a report by a local authority or other person appointed under this subsection shall form part of the expenses of the action and be defrayed by such party to the action as the court may direct, and the court may certify the amount of the expenses so incurred."

RESTRICTIONS ON THE REMOVAL OF A CHILD

When a Custodianship Order is Pending

117. If a child has had his home with the applicants for a custodianship order in respect of him for at least three years (this may be a continuous period or an aggregate period of three years), then no one is entitled to remove the child against the will of the applicant except with the leave of the court, or under authority conferred by any enactment or because of the arrest of the child (section 41* in relation to England and Wales, section 51* in relation to Scotland). This restriction applies equally to a local authority where the child was either in its care before he began to have his home with the applicants or remains in the care of the local authority. Thus foster parents who made an application for custodianship in respect of a child who had had his home with them for at least three years would be protected from the natural parents removing the child, or the local authority, unless the local authority could obtain a place of safety order. The time limit of three years may be varied by the Secretary of State by an order approved by both Houses of Parliament, as is the case in all sections where time limits are set. Any person who contravenes section 41* or 51* commits an offence and is liable on conviction to a fine not exceeding £400 or three months imprisonment or both.

118. If a child has been removed from the custody of a person contrary to section 41* or 51* then the person from whose custody the child has been removed may apply to an authorised court to obtain an order that the child be returned

to him (section 42(1)*) in relation to England and Wales, section 52(1)* in relation to Scotland). Where the applicant suspects that a person is going to remove the child from his custody contrary to section 41* or 51* he may apply to an authorised court for an order that the person shall not remove the child (section 42(2)*, 52(2)*). In England and Wales only, where the court grants an order under section 42(1)*, if the application is granted in the High Court or the county court, the court may order an officer of the court to search any premises specified in the order, and if the child is found the officer of the court shall return him to the applicant (subs. (3)*). If a justice of the peace is satisfied that there are reasonable grounds for believing that a child to whom an order under subsection (1)* relates is in premises specified in information laid before him on oath, then he may issue a search warrant authorising a constable to search the premises for a child, and if he finds the child he shall return him to the applicant (subs.(4)*).

When a Custodianship Order has been Granted

119. The custodian is entitled to the actual custody of the child and this right is enforceable against anyone who has actual custody of the child against the custodian's will. Section 43* sets out the procedure whereby a custodian who is entitled to the actual custody of a child by virtue of an order made in the magistrates' court may enforce his right to actual custody by serving a copy of the custodianship order on the person who has custody of the child.

POWER OF THE COURT TO MAKE A SUPERVISION ORDER OR A CARE ORDER UPON AN APPLICATION FOR CUSTODIANSHIP

120. Where a court is considering an application for custodianship it may decide to make a supervision order or a care order in certain circumstances. It is given power to do this in section 34(4)* which provides that section 2 of the Guardianship Act 1973, subsections (2), (3), (4) and (6), relate to applications for custodianship orders are they apply to

applications under section 9 of the Guardianship of Minors Act 1971. These provisions only apply to a child who is under the age of 16. The court has power to make a superivision order to a specified local authority or to a probation officer if there are "exceptional circumstances making it desirable that the minor shall be under the supervision of an independent person." If there are "exceptional circumstances making it impracticable or undesirable for the minor to be entrusted to either of the parents or to any other individual" the court may make an order committing the care of the child to a specified local authority. Before making the care order however the court must inform the local authority of what it proposes to do and must hear any representations from the authority on this. If the court does commit the child to the care of the local authority, it has the power to order the parents to make payments towards the maintenance of their child having regard to the means of the parent. Where during the hearing of the application the court adjourns the hearing for more than seven days it may make an interim order as to maintenance payments or custody or access. Such interim orders cannot last for longer than three months and cease to have effect on the making of a final order. Similar provisions as to the making of a supervision order or a care order apply on an application for custody in Scotland under section 11 of the Guardianship Act 1973 as amended by section 48(3)* of the 1975 Act.

121. Supervision and care orders made under the provisions of section 34(4)* must be distinguished from such orders made under the Children and Young Persons Act 1969. In relation to orders made under this section, sections 3 and 4 of the Guardianship Act 1973 apply. Section 3 provides in relation to supervision orders that the order shall cease to have effect when the child reaches the age of 16. It makes provision for the selection of a probation officer to supervise the child. It gives the custodian or the probation officer or officer of the local authority the right to apply to the court for a variation or discharge of the order. Section 4 sets out additional provisions in relation to care orders made under section 34(4)*. If the court makes such a care order it shall commit the child to the care of the local authority in whose area the child was resident

before being so committed. Before it makes such an order the court shall inform the local authority and hear any representations from the local authority concerning the making of the order, including representations as to payments to the local authority. Once such a care order is made the order takes effect as though the child were in care under section 1 of the Children Act 1948 with certain exceptions. The child shall remain in the care of the local authority despite any claim by a parent or other person (section 4(5) of the Guardianship Act 1973). Where the order is made by the High Court, the court may make directions concerning the provision of accommodation for the child. The local authority may not arrange for the emigration of the child. Each parent or guardian of a child who is committed to the care of the local authority under this section has a duty to inform the authority of any change of address, and if they fail to do this without reasonable excuse they shall be liable on conviction to a fine not exceeding £10 (section 4(6) of the Guardianship Act 1973).

THE MAKING OF A CUSTODIANSHIP ORDER

Instead of an Adoption Order

122. In certain circumstances the court may make a custodianship order even though the applicants were applying for an adoption order. In the case of an adoption application by relatives or by the husband or wife of the mother or father of the child, either alone or jointly with their spouse, provided that the requirements concerning consent have been satisfied both in the case of an adoption order and a Convention adoption order, the court may make a custodianship order if it feels that either the child's welfare would not be better safeguarded and promoted by the making of an adoption order than a custodianship order, or it would be appropriate to make a custodianship order in the applicant's favour. If the appliction is made jointly by the mother or father of the child and her husband or his wife, the court in deciding to make a custodianship order shall direct the application to be treated as if made by the father's wife or the mother's husband alone (section 37*). The section also gives the court power to make a

custodianship order on the application for an adoption order by a person, or a married couple, who are not relatives of the child or the husband or wife of the mother or the father of the child where the requirements as to consent are satisfied but the court feels a custodianship order was more appropriate. This provision together with the provision prohibiting applications for adoption where the child is the subject of a custody order made in the divorce courts bring into effect the Houghton Committee recommendation that adoption by relatives should be prohibited except in exceptional circumstances (see para. 47).

123. Once the court treats the application as an application for custodianship then all the provisions of Part II* of the Act apply to the application with the exception of section 40* (duty of the applicant to give notice of the application to the local authroity). In the circumstances the court would already have before it a report prepared by the adoption agency or local authority as the adoption application procedure requires this.

124. The provisions of section 37(1)* and (1A)* do not apply to applications to adopt made by the mother or father of the child alone (subs. (4)*). As we have seen the mother or father of a child cannot apply for a custodianship order (section 33(4)*) and an adoption order can only be made in exceptional circumstances in favour of the mother or father alone (section 11(4)*).

Similar provision apply in Scotland by virtue of section 53*.

Instead of an Order under the Guardianship Acts

125. Where a mother or father of the child have applied for custody and maintenance under section 9 of the Guardianship of Minors Act 1971 and the court is of the opinion that the legal custody of the child should be given to a person other than the mother or father of the child it may direct that the application shall be treated as though it were an application for a custodianship order under section 33* and as though the applicant were qualified to apply for an order under this section, even if this is not the case (section 37(3)*). Again the duty to notify the local authority of the application does not apply under section 40*, but all the other provisions of Part II*

of the Act apply and the court has power to request a report
from the local authority under section 39*.

PROVISIONS FOR ACCESS AND MAINTENANCE

126. The Act contains broadly based provisions for access
and maintenance whilst a custodianship order is in force. The
child's mother or father have a right to apply to the court for
such provision as the court thinks fit for access to the child
(section 34(1)(*a**). The custodian may apply to the court
requiring the child's mother or father to make such payments
towards the child's maintenance as the court thinks reasonable
(section 34(1)(*b*)* in relation to England and Wales; a similar
right already exists in relation to Scotland). But an order
cannot be made under this subsection requiring the father of
an illegitimate child to make payments to the child's
custodian, (section 34(3)*). The custodian has a right to apply
for an affiliation order under section 45* of the Act and this
exclusion under section 34* is to prevent an alternative
procedure being used in these circumstances from that laid
down in the Affiliation Proceedings Act 1957. The custodian
or the child's mother or father have a right to apply to the
court to vary any order made under any other enactment
requiring the child's mother or father to make a contribution
towards the child's maintenance, either by altering the amount
of the contributions or by substituting the custodian for the
person to whom contributions were ordered to be made
(section 34(1)(*d*)*). The child's mother or father may apply to
the court to revoke an order made by any court, otherwise than
this section, requiring the applicant to contribute towards the
child's maintenance (section 34(1)(*c*)*). A local authority may
make payments to the custodian except where he is the
husband or she is the wife of a parent of the child (section
34(5)* in relation to England and Wales, section 50* in relation
to Scotland). This would enable a local authority to continue
making payments to foster parents who successfully applied for
a custodianship order in respect of a child that was in care.

127. An order for the payment of money under section 34*
may be enforced in the same way as an affiliation order
(section 43(3)*). Section 43(2)* lays a duty on anyone under an

obligation to make payments under section 34* to give notice of change of address to any person specified in the order. Failure to comply with this requirement could mean a fine on conviction not exceeding £10.

DISPUTES BETWEEN JOINT CUSTODIANS

128. In the case of two persons who have parental rights and duties in respect of a child vested in them jointly by a custodianship order, or by a step-parent becoming a custodian and holding legal custody jointly with the parent of the child, and who cannot agree on the exercise of a parental right and duty, an application may be made to an authorised court asking it to make an order concerning the exercise of that right or performance of that duty as it thinks fit (section 38*). By virtue of section 39* the court has the power to request a report from the local authority or a probation officer in relation to a dispute between joint custodians.

REVOCATION AND VARIATION OF ORDERS

129. Unlike an adoption order a custodianship order may be revoked or varied. Section 35* provides that an application to revoke a custodianship order may be made by the custodian, the mother, father, guardian of the child, or any local authority in England and Wales. If the custodianship order is revoked by the court then any order as to access or maintenance made under the provisions of section 34* automatically cease to have effect (section 35(5)*) and the legal custody of the child revests in the person who had custody before the order was made subject to the provisons of section 36* (see para. 132). Again the court has power under section 39* to request a report from the local authority or a probation officer. A custodianship order and any order made under section 34* cease to have effect when the child reaches the age of 18 (section 35(6)*).

130. Subsection (2)* imposes restrictions on persons who have previously unsuccessfully applied for revocation as clearly a string of applications for revocation could detract from the security which a custodianship order should in theory give a

child and his custodian. The subsection provides that a court shall not hear an application for revocation of a custodianship order where the applicant had previously unsuccessfully applied to that court or any other court, unless, either in refus-refusing the previous application the court directed that this subsection should not apply, or it appears to the court that there has been a change of circumstances or that for any other reason it directs that it is proper to proceed with the application.

131. The custodian of the child is empowered to apply for the revocation or variation of any order made under section 34* in respect of the child (section 35(3)*). There is also a general right for any other person on whose application an order under section 34* was made or who was required by such an order to contribute towards the maintenance of the child to apply to an authorised court for the revocation or variation of that order (section 35(4)*).

132. Before revoking a custodianship order the court has a duty to ascertain who would have the legal custody of the child if the order were revoked in accordance with the provisions of section 36*. If it appears to the court that the child would not be in the legal custody of any person, then the court shall, if it revokes the custodianship order, commit the child to the care of the local authority. The provisions of section 4 of the Guardianship Act apply to such care orders, as they do to orders made under section 34* committing the child to the care of the local authority. Before deciding who would have the legal custody of the child if the order were revoked the court shall, unless it has sufficient information before it already, request the local authority or a probation officer to prepare a report for the court, either orally or in writing, on the desirability of the child returning to the legal custody of any individual. The provisions of subsections (2) to (6) of section 6 of the Guardianship Act 1973 apply to these reports as they do to reports given under section 39* (see para. 114). If on considering the desirability of the child returning to the legal custody of any individual it decides that this would not be desirable then it may commit the child to the care of the local authority in accordance with the provisions of section 4 of the Guardianship Act 1973. If the court decides that it is desirable for the child to be in the legal custody of that person, but that

it is also desirable in the child interests for him to be under the supervision of an independent person, then the court may on revoking the order, order that the child should be under the supervision of the local authority or of a probation officer. Should such a supervision order be made the provisions of section 3 of the Guardianship Act 1973 apply to the order (see para. 121).

IS CUSTODIANSHIP AN ACCEPTABLE ALTERNATIVE TO ADOPTION

133. Custodianship will give foster parents legal security in their relationship with their foster child and as an alternative to adoption by relatives, will prevent the child's links with his natural relatives being broken as they would be by adoption.

134. However, serious criticism has been levelled at the concept of custodianship particularly in relation to its use by foster parents. Foster parents will probably find the concept of custodianship attractive in that it will prevent natural parents from removing a child who has been in their care for an aggregate period of three years or more whilst it will not preclude them from continuing to receive an allowance from the local authority (section 34(5)*). It may in this way prevent some "tug of love" cases. But there is a real danger that natural parents whose children have to come into care may feel that their own rights in relation to the child are so threatened by this new power which foster parents will have that they will remove their child from care before the three-year period has elapsed for no other reason than to prevent a custodianship application. Such an action would not be in the interests of the child. It is also possible that a natural parent will insist that a child coming into care must be placed in a children's home rather than a foster home to avoid the possibility of a custodianship application. We know that good foster care is for many children the best form of substitute care and placement in a children's home could well be against the child's best interests. There is also the danger that parents will avoid asking the local authority to receive their child into care because they are frightened they will lose the child and they will resort to placing their children with a private foster

parent. Some private foster parents can be highly unsuitable
and such arrangements again may not be in the child's best
interests. Neither is there anything to prevent a private foster
parent from applying for custodianship. If a custodianship
order is made to local authority foster parents the child ceases
to be in care and the foster parents are no longer subject to the
Boarding Out Regulations. This will mean that the foster
parent's will no longer have regular visits from a social worker
who can give them professional advice and support in dealing
with problems relating to the child. There is a danger that
those foster parents who resent the interference of the local
authority, and those who may not be the most suitable foster
parents are the very ones who choose to apply for a
custodianship order. The local authority could oppose their
application but will have to show that the order will not be in
the interests of the child, which could be difficult to prove if
the child has lived with the applicants for some years.
Hopefully the power of the court to make a supervision order
will ensure that those foster parents who need social work
support will continue to receive it.

135. There is some doubt as to whether custodionship will be
an acceptable alternative to adoption for relatives. It will not
conceal the reality of the child's family background and may
thus be unacceptable to some relatives on this ground. In the
case of adoptions by parent and step-parent it may prove even
less acceptable. There will be no new birth certificate or
change of the child's name to the new family name. In the case
of a legitimate child the parent and step-parent will have to
return to the domestic court for a variation of custody order
and some would find this a painful reminder of old conflicts
and hesitate to apply for this reason. For many parents
adoption seems more socially acceptable than custody
proceedings. For these reasons custodianship is unlikely to be
as popular with relatives as adoption.

136. It seems then that custodianship is a mixed blessing.
Whilst giving foster parents who apply some legal security in
respect of children they have in their care, custodianship could
have a serious effect on fostering as a form of substitute care
and on its use by local authorities. As an alternative to
adoption for relatives it may be little used.

10 Amendments to the Children Act 1948

137. Part III of the Act makes amendments to and extends the legislation relating to children in the care of local authorities and voluntary organisations. It was realised that this Act was likely to be the only opportunity that Parliament would have for many years to amend legislation relating to children and for this reason the scope of the Bill was extended considerably by the many additional amendments which were added as it passed through Parliament. This chapter deals with amendments to the Children Act 1948 and related amendments and the following chapter deals with amendments to the Children and Young Persons Act 1969. Similarly the Act amends the Scottish law relating to children and these amendments are set out in Chapter 12. The amendments and additions to the Children Act 1948 cover five main areas. The general duty of local authorities in care cases is changed. A new restriction on parents removing children who have been in care under section 1 of the 1948 Act for six months or more is included. Section 2 of the 1948 Act is redrafted and a new ground on which local authorities can assume parental rights and duties is introduced. The position of voluntary organisations is considerably strengthened in relation to children in their care. A new procedure is set out in section 67* to enable children to be recovered who are in care under the provisions of the 1948 Act and unlawfully removed.

GENERAL DUTY OF LOCAL AUTHORITIES IN CARE CASES

138. The general duty of local authorities when making decisions in relation to children in their care, previously set out in section 12 of the Children Act 1948 and modified by section 27(2) of the Children and Young Persons Act 1969 is replaced by section 59 of the 1975 Act, in relation to England and Wales. Previously the duty of the local authority according to

section 12 of the 1948 Act was to further the best interests of a child in their care and "to afford him opportunity for the proper development of his character and abilities." Section 59 substitutes a new subsection for section 12(1) which provides:

"In reaching any decision relating to a child in their care, a local authority shall give first consideration to the need to safeguard and promote the welfare of the child throughout his childhood; and shall so far as practicable ascertain the wishes and feelings of the child regarding the decision and give due consideration to them, having regard to his age and understanding."

It is clear that this duty is similar to the duty to safeguard and promote the welfare of the child in adoption proceedings set out in section 3 of the Act. The second limb of the subsection gives a child some say in decisions made about his welfare if he is old enough to understand the nature and the implications of the decision. This represents yet another small step in the movement which the Act makes towards the concept of children having rights independently of their parents or the local authority.

139. The requirement that a local authority shall give first consideration to the welfare of the child is modified however by the new subsection (1A) which section 59 inserts into section 12 of the 1948 Act. This provides that:

"If it appears to the local authority that it is necessary, for the purpose of protecting members of the public, to exercise their powers in relation to a particular child in their care in a manner which may not be consistent with their duty under the foregoing subsection, the authority may, notwithstanding that duty, act in that manner."

As the duty under this section relates not only to children in care under the provisions of the 1948 Act but also to a child who is in care because he is the subject of a care order made under the provisions of the Children and Young Persons Act 1969, subsection (1A) ensures that although first consideration should be given to the welfare of the child this is not the overriding consideration. There are cases of children who are made the subject of care orders for the purpose of protecting members of the public, as in the case of a child who has committed a long string of criminal offences. It may not be in the interests of the welfare of the child, and would almost certainly be against his wishes, to be removed from the local community and placed in the care of the local authority, nevertheless the local authority will be able to do this under subsection (1A) despite the provisions of section 12(1) of the 1948 Act.

RESTRICTIONS ON THE REMOVAL OF A CHILD FROM CARE

140. A child who is placed in the care of the local authority voluntarily by parents under section 1 of the 1948 Act could be removed by them from care at any time, no matter how long the child had been in care. This was irrespective of whether it was in the child's interests to return home. The Houghton Committee considered the position of children in the care of local authorities and voluntary societies, and in particular those children in long stay foster homes who are reclaimed by their parents at very short notice. The Committee recognised that this is a complex problem where the law has to strive to keep a balance between the rights of the natural parents, the rights of the child and the rights of the foster parents. One of their recommendations was that children who have been in the care of the local authority under section 1 of the 1948 Act for 12 months or more should be protected from being suddenly removed from care by their parents. They recommended that the law should require parents to give 28 days notice to the local authority that they intend to remove their child from care.

141. Section 56* of the Act gives effect to part of the Committee's recommendation by inserting a new subsection (3A)* into section 1 of the 1948 Act, but requires the child to have been in care for 6 months or more, not 12 months as in the original recommendation. Once the child has been in the care of the local authority for six months or more the parents must give the local authority 28 days' notice of their intention to remove the child, unless the authority gives their consent to the child being removed at an earlier date. If a parent or guardian removes the child without such notice being given or before the expiry of the 28 day period he will be deemed to

have committed an offence under section 3(8) of the 1948 Act and will be liable on conviction to a fine not exceeding £400 or to a term of imprisonment not exceeding three months or both (these penalties have been increased by para. 4 of Schedule 3 to the 1975 Act).

142. The setting of this time limit at 6 months was the subject of considerable debate during the passage of the Bill through Parliament. At one time the limit was set at 12 months as in the original recommendation, and later there was sliding scale of time limits but eventually the time limit of 6 months was introduced as an acceptable compromise between the differing points of view. As with other time limits in the Act the period of 6 months may be changed by the Secretary of State by an order approved by each House of Parliament (subs. (3B)* of section 1 of the 1948 Act, as substituted by section 56* of the 1975 Act).

143. This provision will not affect the large numbers of children who come into care for short periods but are designed to safeguard the interests of children who have been in care for 6 months or more and allow for a planned re-introduction to their home environment. It is hoped that it will prevent sudden or shortlived removals from care which could be damaging to the child. At first sight it does not seem to represent a serious threat to the rights of natural parents. The 28 day period would however give a local authority time, if it were so minded and if there were grounds, to assume parental rights under section 2 of the 1948 Act. Some parents might see the requirement to give notice as an infringement of their rights and remove the child from care before the 6 months has elapsed for no other reason than to avoid the requirement.

Extension of this provision to voluntary societies

144. Section 56* also inserts a new section into the 1948 Act, section 33A*, which provides that the new subsection (3A)* in section 1 of the 1948 Act shall apply to children in the care of voluntary homes or boarded out by them, notwithstanding the fact that they are not in the care of the local authority under section 1. The same penalties for removing a child without giving the required period of notice apply here as they do to section 1(3)A1)*.69)

ASSUMPTION OF PARENTAL RIGHTS AND DUTIES BY LOCAL AUTHORITIES

145. Section 2 of the 1948 Act which provides for the assumption of parental rights by a local authority in respect of a child in their care under section 1 is replaced by a new section 2* enacted in section 57* of the 1975 Act. This follows the recommendations of the Houghton Committee who carried out surveys of children reclaimed from care. In a study of children removed from the care of the local authority against the authority's strong advice it was found that children are rarely removed precipitantly from the care of those authorities who made full use of their powers under section 2. Although the Committee felt that some local authorities did not use their powers under section 2 as assiduously as they might, they agreed that the local authority's powers under section 2 were not always adequate. They felt it would be an advantage for a local authority to be able to assume parental rights in respect of any child who had been in their care under section 1 for a continuous period of three years. They also recommended that where parental rights have been assumed by a resolution against one of the parents and the other parent requests that the child be allowed home, the local authority should be allowed to retain the child in their care if the parent against whom the resolution stood was a member of the household to which the child would return.

146. Both these recommendations are given effect in the rewritten section 2* which is substituted for the existing section 2 by section 57* of the 1975 Act. The rewritten section 2* tidies up the old section 2 which had been amended by section 48 of the Children and Young Persons Act 1963 and sets out the grounds upon which a local authority may assume parental rights more clearly. The new section 2* uses the concept of "parental rights and duties" which is used throughout the 1975 Act and defined in section 85 of the Act. When the local authority makes a resolution under section 2(1)* it assumes all the rights and duties that the parent of a legitimate child would have with the exception of the right to consent to the child's adoption, or to an order freeing the child for adoption or to an application under section 25* of the Act (Adoption of

children abroad)(section 2(11)*). The two new grounds on which the local authority may resolve that the parental rights and duties shall vest in them in respect of a child in their care under section 2(1)* are:

"(c) that a resolution under paragraph (b) of this sub-section is in force in relation to one parent of the child who is, or is likely to become, a member of the household comprising the child and his other parent; or

(d) that throughout the three years preceding the passing of the resolution the child has been in the care of a local authority under the foregoing section, or partly in the care of a local authority and partly in the care of a voluntary organisation ...."

147. The procedure regarding the giving of notice to the parents or guardian of the parental rights resolution is similar to that set out in the former section 2. Every notice given by the local authority must inform the person on whom it is served of his right to object to the resolution within one month, and the effect of any objection made by him (subs.(3)*). A local authority must serve this notice by registered post or recorded delivery although a person may give notice of his objection to the resolution by ordinary post (subs.(7)*). If a parent does object to the resolution it lapses within 14 days unless the local authority complains to the juvenile court having jurisdiction in their area during this 14 days. Once this has been done the resolution will not lapse until the court hearing (subs.(5)*). The court has power to order that the resolution does not lapse if it is satisfied on three grounds:

"(a) that the grounds mentioned in subsection (1) of this section on which the local authority purported to pass the resolution were made out, and

(b) that at the time of the hearing there continued to be grounds on which a resolution under subsection (1) of this section could be founded, and

(c) that it is in the interests of the child to do so."

While a resolution is in force under subsection (1)(b)*(c)* or (d)* of this section a parent or guardian, who but for the resolution would have had parental rights and duties is not entitled to remove the child from the care of the local authority (subs.(6)*). A resolution made under section 2* ceases to have effect if a guardian is appointed under section 5 of the Guardianship of Minors Act 1971, if the child is adopted, or is the subject of an order freeing him for adoption or an order under section 25 enabling him to be adopted abroad (subs.(8)*). If a child is made the subject of a custodianship order the custodian becomes entitled to the legal custody of the child but the resolution does not lapse and should the custodianship order be revoked the local authority would again be entitled to the legal custody of the child. (The definition of "legal custody" is discussed in paragraph 104.)

148. Once again the time limit of three years set out in section 2(1)(*d*)* may be altered by the Secretary of State by an order which has been approved by each House of Parliament. The British Association of Social Workers strongly opposed the use of time limits which the Act makes. The introduction of a new ground on which parental rights could be assumed after a child has been in care for three years was felt by them to be particularly dangerous in that it might lead to parents impulsively removing their children from care to avoid the three year limit. The increase in power which the new provision gives local authorities might frighten parents into making alternative and possibly inferior arrangements for the care of their children. The Association of British Adoption Agencies, on the other hand, have favoured the use of time limits as they focus attention on the importance of the passage of time in a child's life. Too often a child remains in long term care because the resources are not there for social workers to work towards the rehabilitation of the child with his parents and too often decisions affecting the long term welfare of a child are delayed or made by default.

Right of appeal to the High Court

149. The rights of natural parents are safeguarded to some extent in that they are given the right to appeal to the High Court of the juvenile court confirms a parental rights resolution or refuses to terminate such a resolution (section 58* of the Act which inserts a new section 4A* into the 1948 Act). Conversely this right also applies to local authorities.

Right of the court to appoint a guardian ad litem

150. In any proceedings in the juvenile court under section 2(5) of the 1948 Act (application by the local authority to confirm a parental rights resolution) or section 4(3) (application by a parent or guardian to the court to terminate such a resolution) or section 4A* (see para. 149) the juvenile court or the High Court may appoint a guardian *ad litem* to safeguard the interests of the child. As in other cases where a guardian *ad litem* is appointed the guardian has a duty to safeguard the interests of the child in the manner prescribed by rules of court. The guardian *ad litem's* report given in such hearings is governed by section 6 of the Guardianship Act 1973 as amended by section 90 of the 1975 Act (see para. 114). These provisions are set out in section 58* of the Act which inserts a new section, 4B* into the 1948 Act.

STRENGTHENING OF THE POSITION OF VOLUNTARY ORGANISATIONS IN RELATION TO CHILDREN IN THEIR CARE

151. As we have seen in paragraph 143 a parent will not be allowed to remove a child from the care of a voluntary organisation without giving 28 days' notice once the child has been in its care for six months or more. The position of voluntary societies is further strengthened by sections 60* to 63* of the new Act. Up until the 1975 Act voluntary societies were not in a comparable position to local authorities in relation to children in their care. Section 60* however enables a local authority to assume parental rights and duties in respect of a child who is in the care of a voluntary organisation within its area, provided that the organisation is an incorporated body and the child is not in the care of a local authority and one of the conditions set out in section 2(1)* of the 1948 Act are satisfied in respect of the child. The child must be living within the area of the local authority, either in a voluntary home or with foster parents with whom he has been boarded out by the organisation, and the organisation must have requested the local authority to pass the resolution. The effect of the resolution is similar to that made under section 2*

in that it vests the legal custody of the child in the voluntary organisation but it does not give the organisation the right to consent to the child's adoption, or to an order freeing the child for adoption or to an application made under section 25* of the 1975 Act. The procedure by which such a resolution is made and the requirements regarding the giving of notice to each parent or guardian are the same as those set out in section 2* of the 1948 Act (section 63*). The parent may object to the making of the resolution in the same way as he can under section 2,* in which case the juvenile court must confirm the resolution if it is not to lapse.

152. The local authority is given the power, by section 61*, to resolve that the parental rights and duties in respect of a child who is the subject of a resolution under section 60* shall vest in itself rather than the voluntary organisation if this appears to be in the child's interests. The local authority must inform each parent, guardian or custodian of the child whose whereabouts are known within seven days by notice in writing of the passing of this resolution under section 61*. A parent, guardian or custodian who is given notice in this way may apply to a juvenile court in the area on the ground that either there was no ground for the making of the resolution or that the resolution should in the interests of the child be determined (section 63*). As in the new section 4A* of the 1948 Act an appeal lies to the High Court against a decision of the juvenile court under this section (section 63(3)*). Moreover the power of the juvenile court or the High Court to appoint a guardian *ad litem* under the new section 4B* of the 1948 Act also applies to proceedings under this section (section 63(4)*).

RECOVERY OF CHILDREN REMOVED FROM CARE

153. Section 67* of the Act introduces new powers to recover children who are in the care of the local authority and who are the subject of a resolution under section 2 of the 1948 Act who either abscond or are taken away from the accommodation provided for them by the local authority. It also covers those cases where the local authority has allowed a child who is the subject of a section 2 resolution to be in the charge of a parent, guardian, relative or friend, and where the local authority has

served a notice on that person under section 49 of the Children and Young Persons Act 1963 requiring him to return the child, and he has failed to do so. In these circumstances if a justice of the peace is satisfied by information on oath that there are "reasonable grounds" for believing that a person specified in the information can produce a child to whom this section applies, he may issue a summons directing that person to attend the magistrates' court and produce the child (subs.(2)*). Moreover if the justice of the peace is satisfied that there are "reasonable grounds" for believing that the child is in premises specified in the information he may issue a search warrant to an officer of the local authority in whose care the child is to search these premises. If the officer then finds the child he may be placed in accommodation provided for him by the local authority in accordance with the 1948 Act (subs.(3)*). A person who without reasonable excuse does not comply with a summons issued under this section to produce a child is guilty of an offence and is liable on conviction to a fine not exceeding £100.

11 Amendments to the Children and Young Persons Act 1969

Part III of the Act also contains amendments to the Children and Young Persons Act 1969. One of the most significant of these amendments in the introduction of separate representation for a child in court where there is a conflict of interests between a child and his parents in certain proceedings under the Act. Section 1 of the 1969 Act is amended to include a new ground for care proceedings, with the effect that an order may be made under that section where a person who has been convicted of one of the offences listed in Schedule 1 to the Children and Young Persons Act 1933 is or may become a member of the same household as the child in respect of whom the proceedings are brought. The Act also contains provisions concerning the administration of supervision orders, and the recovery of a child missing from a place of safety. New regulations are to be brought in concerning the making of unruly certificates and the Secretary of State is given power to make grants to local authorities to provide secure accommodation in community schools.

SEPARATE REPRESENTATION OF PARENT AND CHILD BEFORE THE COURT

154. Before the 1975 Act there was no legal recognition that it might be in a child's interests to be separately represented from his parents in court proceedings which related to the child. Even in care proceedings where allegations were made about the parent's conduct towards the child the child had no right to be separately represented, and his representative was also the parent's representative. Moreover the local authority social worker who prepares a report for the court in such circumstances looks at the family situation as a whole and not at the interests of the child in particular. It has been

recognised in recent years that parents are not necessarily the best people to represent their own children especially in proceedings where the parents' suitability is being challenged and with this realisation the idea of separate representation fo children in such proceedings has grown. The Maria Colwel case is one which must spring to everyone's mind as an example of a situation where an independent spokesman representing the child's circumstances and feelings to the court might have prevented the discharge of the care order, and thereby avoided the ensuing tragedy.

155. The 1975 Act introduces the idea of separate representation for the child, but only in certain circumstances not, as many had hoped, in all proceedings relating to a child As we have seen the Act gives the court power to appoint a guardian *ad litem* to safeguard the child's interests in adoption proceedings and in proceedings in the juvenile court or High Court in applications to confirm or terminate a resolution made under section 2* of the Children Act 1948 or appeal from such hearings. Section 64* of the Act inserts two new sections after section 32 of the Children and Young Person Act 1969, sections 32A* and 32B*. Section 32A* provides tha in care proceedings under section 1 of the 1969 Act, or in applications to discharge a supervision order under section 15(1) or a care order under section 21(2) of that Act or appeal from the dismissal of such appliction to the Crown Court, if i appears that there may be a conflict of interests on any matter relevant to the proceedings between the child and the parent or guardian, the court may order that the parent or guardian shall not be treated as prepresenting the child for the purpose of the proceedings, unless the court is satisfied that to do so is unnecessary (section 32A(1)*). Once such an order is made i also applies to any appeal to the Crown Court which arise from those proceedings (section 32A(3)*). If an application to the court to revoke a supervision order under section 15(1) or a care order under section 21(2) is unopposed the court mus order that no parent or guardian shall be treated as representing the interests of the child, unless the court i satisfied that it is unnecessary to do this (section 32A(2)* Section 32B* then provides that once the court has made such an order under section 32A it must appoint a guardian *ad*

litem as well to safeguard the interests of the child in the proceedings, again with the proviso that it need not do so if it is satisfied that this is unnecessary. The guardian *ad litem* will be selected from a panel of persons to be set up by the Secretary of State in accordance with section 103 of the Act. The duty of the guardian *ad litem* will be to safeguard the interests of the child in the manner prescribed by rules of court (section 32B(3)*).

156. These provisions will go further towards safeguarding the interests of the child than the law allows at present, although some would argue that by not providing for separate representation in all proceedings relating to a child the reforms of the 1975 Act do not go far enough. Nevertheless these additional duties which guardian *ad litem* work will involve for social workers will mean that over-burdened social work manpower resources will be under yet more pressure. The Act does not prohibit the guardian *ad litem* from being selected from the same local authority as the social worker involved with the case, but if this were to happen it could appear to parents that social workers were colluding against them. There was some feeling in Parliament that a paid court official trained in social work, such as "Justice" recommended in their report on *Parental Rights and Duties in Custody Suits* (1975) would be a more suitable person to represent the interests of the child impartially but this solution was rejected.

RIGHT OF THE PARENT TO LEGAL AID

157. If the court makes an order under section 32A* of the Children and Young Persons Act 1969 ordering separate representation for the child, section 65* of the 1975 Act amends the Legal Aid Act 1974 to ensure that the parent or guardian or any person who has custody of the child (for example a custodian) has a right to apply for legal aid for the purpose of taking part in the proceedings. By this provision the Act seeks to maintain a balance of rights between the parties and should go some way towards safeguarding the rights of inarticulate parents.

NEW GROUND FOR CARE PROCEEDINGS UNDER SECTION 1 OF THE 1969 ACT

158. A new ground for care proceedings under section 1 of the 1969 Act is set out in Schedule 3, paragraph 67. This provides that the following paragraph is inserted after paragraph (*b*) in section 1(2):

"(*bb*) it is probable that the condition set out in paragraph (a) of this subsection will be satisfied in his case, having regard to the fact that a person who has been convicted of an offence mentioned in Schedule 1 to the Act of 1933 is, or may become, a member of the same household as the child;"

The offences set out in Schedule 1 to the Children and Young Persons Act 1933 are murder, manslaughter, infanticide or any offence involving an assault, either physical or sexual, against a child. The offence will not have to have been committed against the child in respect of whom the proceedings are brought. To satisfy the court that there are grounds for making an order under section 1 of the 1969 Act under this new paragraph three elements will have to be proved. First, that a person has committed an offence listed in Schedule 1 to the 1933 Act. Secondly, that the person is a member of the same household as the child in respect of whom the proceedings are brought or that the person is likely to become a member of that household. Thirdly, that the child is likely to be ill-treated or neglected within the terms of section 1(2)(a). The fact that a person has committed an offence which falls within Schedule 1 is not therefore grounds in its own right for the making of an order under section 1, but having established that such an offence has been committed it is only necessary to establish that illtreatment or neglect is "probable." This amendment was introduced into the Act in its latter stages in Parliament as a result of comments made by the Association of Directors of Social Services and the results of the Auckland case inquiry which illustrated the need for such an amendment to the Act.

AMENDMENTS RELATING TO THE
ADMINISTRATION OF SUPERVISION ORDERS

159. The Committee of Inquiry Report into the Maria Colwell case emphasised the need for regulations governing the administration of supervision orders, although Olive Stevenson dissented from this point of view in her minority report. The Committee felt that if there had been regulations governing the administration of supervision orders rather than just a duty laid on the supervisor to "advise, assist and befriend the supervised person" the supervision of Maria might not have broken down in the way it did.

160. Schedule 3 to the 1975 Act contains two amendments to provisions concerning supervision orders. Paragraph 68 of the Schedule inserts a new section, section 11A into the 1969 Act which empowers the Secretary of State to make regulations with respect to the exercise by a local authority of their functions where a supervision order has been made as a result of care proceedings under section 1 of the Act or as a result of an application to discharge a care order brought under section 21(2) of that Act.

161. Schedule 3, paragraph 69 inserts a new subsection into section 21 of the 1969 Act. This new subsection requires that the juvenile court, when hearing an application to discharge a care order, shall not discharge the care order and replace it by a supervision order unless it is satisfied that the child will receive the necessary care and control whether through the making of the supervision order or otherwise.

RECOVERY OF A CHILD MISSING FROM
A PLACE OF SAFETY

162. Section 68* of the Act extends the existing powers given by section 32 of the 1969 Act to recover a child who is absent without authority from a place at which he is required to live. Section 32 covers absences from a place of safety which are community homes but does not cover absences from other places of safety such as a police station or a hospital. Section 68* gives a constable the right to arrest without a warrant any child who is missing from any place of safety and the power to

conduct that child once again to the place of safety (new subs. (1A)*). The section also gives a magistrates' court the power on receiving information given under oath to issue a search warrant to enable a constable to search premises where the child is believed to be, and if he is found the constable will be able to conduct him to a place of safety in accordance with the power given under subsection (1A*)(subs. 2A*). Under section 32(2) a magistrates' court on receipt of information given on oath that a person can produce a child missing under subsection (1) or (1A)* may issue a summons requiring that person to produce the child. If a person fails to produce the child without reasonable cause he is liable on conviction to a fine not exceeding £100 (penalty increased by section 68*). If a person is convicted of compelling, persuading, inciting or assisting another person to become or continue to be absent under subsection (1) or (1A)* he is liable on conviction to a term of imprisonment not exceeding six months or a fine not exceeding £400 or both (penalty increased from £100 to £400 by section 68*).

UNRULY CERTIFICATES

163. Section 69* of the Act provides that the court shall not certify under section 22(5), section 23(2) or (3) of the 1969 Act that a child is of so unruly a character that he cannot be safely committed to the care of a local authority unless conditions prescribed by order of the Secretary of State are satisfied in relation to the child. This section was inserted in the Act at the last moment and reflects the growing concern about the large numbers of children who are being certified "unruly" and ending up in prison establishments. The section simply gives the Secretary of State an order-making power and it is unlikely that the regulations will be drafted before the Report of the Pack Committee on unruly children is presented to the Home Office in 1976. It is likely that the regulations will make it harder to make unruly certificates, but again the problem here is not one which legislation alone can solve. There are insufficient secure places in community schools and there are insufficient numbers of trained staff and until this problem is tackled the situation will not change appreciably.

GRANTS IN RESPECT OF SECURE ACCOMMODATION

164. Section 71 of the Act inserts a new section after section 64 of the 1969 Act, section 64A, which gives the Secretary of State the power to make grants to local authorities to provide secure accommodation in community schools. This provision is linked with the previous section and is an attempt to stem the growing numbers of children who are committed to prison establishments because of the lack of secure places. Given the present economic recession and the difficulties of staffing secure establishments this provision is only likely to be effective in the long term.

12 Amendments to Legislation relating to Children in Care in Scotland

Part III of the Act is something of a legislative jungle in which extensive amendments are made to the law relating to children in care in both England and Wales and Scotland. To present these amendments in a digestible form the position in England and Wales has been described in the two preceding chapters and this chapter sets out the amendments to the Scottish law made in Part III of the 1975 Act. The Social Work (Scotland) Act 1968 (hereafter called the 1968 Act) is the principal Act governing the position of children in care in Scotland. Many of its provisions parallel those of the Children Act 1948 and the Children and Young Persons Act 1969 but there are differences in terminology and procedures, one of the most significant differences in procedure being the system of children's hearings which do not exist in England and Wales. The amendments to the 1968 Act are for the most part comparable with those to the 1948 and 1969 Acts, although some amendments relate to Scotland alone.

GENERAL DUTY OF LOCAL AUTHORITIES IN CARE CASES

165. The general duty of local authorities when making decisions in relation to children in their care is altered by section 79* of the Act which amends section 20 of the 1968 Act. The new duty requires the local authority in reaching any decision in relation to a child in its care under any enactment to give "first consideration to the need to safeguard and promote the welfare of the child throughout his childhood" and in reaching such decisions the authority shall as far as is

practicable take account of the child's wishes and feelings on the matter having regard to his age and understanding. This new duty of care is substituted for the existing requirement to promote the interests of the child. It brings the duty of care into line with that laid down for adoption proceedings in section 3 of the Act and relates to all children in care, whether they came into care by voluntary arrangement under section 15 or otherwise.

RESTRICTIONS ON THE REMOVAL OF A CHILD FROM CARE

166. If a child is placed in the care of the local authority voluntarily by parents under section 15 of the 1968 Act they could remove the child from care at any time. The Houghton Committee felt that children who had been in care voluntarily for long periods should be protected from being suddenly removed by their parents. They recommended that the parents should be required to give 28 days' notice to the local authority that they intend to remove the child from care if the child has been in care for a year or more. This would enable the child's re-introduction to his home to be planned and avoid sudden or short-lived removals from care which could be damaging to the child.

167. Section 73* gives effect to this recommendation by inserting a new subsection into section 15 of the 1968 Act, subsection (3A)*, but requires the child to have been in care under the section for six months or more not 12 months as in the original recommendation. Once the child has been in care for six months or more tha parent or guardian must give the local authority 28 days' notice of his intention to remove the child from care. The local authority may consent to the child being removed before the period of 28 days has elapsed, but if such consent is not given and the parent or guardian removes the child without giving notice or before the expiry of the 28 days he will be deemed to have committed an offence under section 17(8). This time limit of six months may be changed by the Secretary of State by an order approved by each House of Parliament (subs.(3B)* of section 15 of the 1968 Act).

Extension of this provision to voluntary societies

168. Section 81* inserts a new section after section 25 of the 1968 Act, section 25A* which provides that the new subsection (3A)* in section 15 of the Act shall apply to a child in the care of a voluntary organisation. For the purposes of this section a child is defined as being in the care of a voluntary organisation if the organisation has provided accommodation in a residential establishment or has boarded out the child. The same penalties for removing a child without giving notice or, without consent, before the 28 days' notice has expired which are set out in section 17(8) of the 1968 Act apply to this section as they do to section 15(3A)*.

ASSUMPTION OF PARENTAL RIGHTS AND POWERS BY A LOCAL AUTHORITY

169. Section 16 of the 1968 Act which provides for the assumption of parental rights and powers by local authorities in respect of children in their care under section 15 is replaced by a new section 16* enacted in section 74* of the 1975 Act. This follows the recommendations of the Houghton Committee who felt that it would be an advantage for a local authority to be able to assume parental rights where a child has been in care for a continuous period of three years under section 15. They also recommended that where parental rights have been assumed against one of the parents and the other parent requests that the child be allowed home, the local authority should be allowed to retain the child in its care if the parent against whom the resolution stood was a member of the household to which the child would return. Both these recommendations are given effect in the rewritten section 16*. The two new grounds on which a local authority may assume parental rights are:

"(*iii*) that a resolution under this subsection is in force in terms of sub-paragraph (*ii*) above in relation to one parent of the child and that parent is, or is likely to become, a member of the household comprising the child and his other parent; or

(*iv*) that throughout the three years preceding the passing of the resolution the child has been in the care of a local authority under section 15 of this Act, or in the

care of a voluntary organisation or partly the one and
partly the other."

170. In the new section 16* the local authority is given the
right to assume parental rights and powers on behalf of a
voluntary organisation, provided that organisation is an
incorporated body or a trust, but certain conditions have to be
satisfied before the local authority can make such a resolution
vesting parental rights in a voluntary organisation. First, it
must be satisfied that the child is not in the care of any local
authority under any enactment. Secondly, it is satisfied that
the resolution in favour of the voluntary organisation is
necessary in the child's interests. Thirdly, the child is living in
the area of the local authority either in a residential
establishment or with foster parents with whom he has been
boarded out by the organisation in whose care he is, and
fourthly, the organisation has requested the local authority to
pass the resolution (subs.(4)*).

171. The procedure regarding the giving of notice to the
parents or guardian of the child is the same as that set out in
section 16 previously. Every notice given by the local authority
must inform the person on whom it is served of his right to
object to the resolution within one month. A local authority
must serve this notice by registered post or recorded delivery
although a person may give notice of his objection to the
resolution by ordinary post (subs.(10)*). If a parent does serve
a counter-notice in writing the local authority must make an
application to the sheriff having jurisdiction within their area
within 14 days otherwise the resolution lapses. Once an
application has been made to the sheriff the resolution will not
lapse until the hearing and the sheriff has power to order that
the resolution shall not lapse if he is satisfied that the grounds
on which the local authority passed the resolution were made
out, that there continued to be grounds for the passing of the
resolution and that the resolution was in the interests of the
child (subs.(8)*).

172. The effect of a parental rights resolution is to vest all
the parental rights in the local authority or voluntary
organisation relating to the child in respect of whom the
resolution is made which vested in the person on whose
account the resolution was passed with the exception that the

local authority or voluntary organisation has no right to consent to or refuse to consent to an order freeing the child for adoption or to the child's adoption (subs.(3)*). A resolution under section 16* ceases to have effect if an adoption order is made, if an order is made freeing a child for adoption or an order made under section 25* of the 1975 Act, or a guardian is appointed under section 4(2A) of the Guardianship of Infants Act 1925 (subs.(11)*).

173. Section 77* of the new Act provides that a court may entertain an application for an adoption order or an order freeing the child for adoption or an order under section 25* of the 1975 Act despite the fact that a local authority or a voluntary organisation have parental rights by virtue of a resolution under section 16* of the 1968 Act (section 18(4A) of the 1968 Act as substituted by section 77* of the 1975 Act).

ASSUMPTION OF PARENTAL RIGHTS BY A LOCAL AUTHORITY WHERE RIGHTS ARE VESTED IN A VOLUNTARY ORGANISATION

174. Section 75* inserts a new section after section 16* of the 1968 Act, section 16A*, which gives a local authority the duty to assume parental rights in certain circumstances where these are vested in a voluntary organisation. The local authority shall in the interests of the welfare of a child living within its area in respect of whom parental rights are vested in a voluntary organisation by virtue of an earlier resolution under section 16*, resolve that the parental rights and powers shall vest in the authority (section 16A(1)*). Within seven days of the passing of such a resolution the local authority must inform the voluntary organisation and any person who but for the resolution would have custody by notice in writing of the transfer of parental rights and powers. A person who but for the resolution and the earlier resolution to the voluntary organisation would have had custody has the right to apply for a hearing before the sheriff having jurisdiction in the area where the applicant resides to decide whether the resolution made under subsection (1)* shall continue to have effect, or the earlier resolution in respect of the voluntary organisation shall continue to have effect, or that the resolution made

under subsection (1)* shall cease to have effect and the applicant shall be granted custody, or that the resolution made under subsection (1)* shall continue to have effect but the applicant shall be allowed to have control of the child (subs.(3)*). The sheriff is also given the right to consider whether the grounds on which the earlier resolution was passed were made out, and if they were not the sheriff may order that the parental rights and powers shall vest in the applicant.

SEPARATE REPRESENTATION OF PARENT AND CHILD BEFORE THE COURT

175. Section 66* inserts a new section after section 34 of the 1968 Act, section 34A* which makes provision for the safeguarding of the interests of a child in any proceedings before a children's hearing or in court proceedings arising from a children's hearing where there is a conflict of interests between the child and his parents. The chairman of the hearing or the sheriff shall consider whether it is necessary to appoint a person for the purpose of safeguarding the interests of the child in the proceedings if there is a conflict of interests between the child and his parents, and may, without prejudice to the existing power to appoint a person to represent the child's interests, appoint such a person.

176. Section 78* which is the Scottish equivalent of section 58* inserts a new section into the 1968 Act, section 18A*, which empowers the sheriff to appoint a person to safeguard the interests of a child in proceedings relating to the assumption of parental rights by a local authority, or applications by a parent or guardian to terminate such resolutions.

AMENDMENTS TO SECTIONS 37 AND 40 OF THE 1968 ACT

177. Section 83 makes amendments to section 37 of the 1968 Act, concerning the making and duration of place of safety orders. A new subsection (1A) is inserted after subsection (1) of section 37 which places a duty on local authorities to investigate cases where they receive information that a child

may need compulsory measures of care, and to pass the information they receive to the reporter to the children's panel if it appears to the local authority that the child may be in need of compulsory measures of care. This subsection adds nothing new to the duty of local authorities, but it sets out the duty more specifically than before.

178. A new subsection is substituted for subsection (2) which extends the circumstances in which a child may be taken to a place of safety. This provides that a constable or any person authorised by a court or a justice of the peace may take a child to a place of safety if any offence of violence (an offence mentioned in Schedule 1 to the Criminal Procedure (Scotland) Act 1975 or under section 21(1) of the Children and Young Persons (Scotland) Act 1937) has been committed or is believed to have been committed against the child or the child is a member of the same household as a child against whom such an offence has been committed, or is likely to become a member of the same household as a person who has committed such an offence, or a child who is likely to be caused unnecessary suffering or serious impairment to his health because there is, or is believed to be, in respect of the child, a lack of parental care. The child may be detained in a place of safety until the case has been brought before a children's hearing. Under subsection (5) a place of safety order, which lasts for 21 days, may be renewed by the reporter for a further 21 days. A new subsection (5A) provides that once a reporter has renewed such a warrant once (*i.e.* after 42 days) the reporter may apply to the sheriff for an extension of the place of safety order if he can show that the child's case cannot be disposed of before the period expires, and that it is in the interests of the child to extend the period. But a warrant authorising detention under subsection (5A) can only be renewed once (subs.5(B)) with the effect that the total period under this section that a place of safety could extend would be 84 days.

179. Section 84 makes amendments to section 40 of the 1968 Act. Under this section a children's hearing could order that a child who had come before it without having previously been placed in a place of safety should be placed in a place of safety if the hearing believed that the child would not attend further hearings. This power is extended by section 84 to allow the

hearing to have the child detained in a place of safety where it believes that it is in the child's interests and where the hearing is not ready to dispose of the case finally. In these circumstances the hearing may issue a warrant requiring the child to be detained in a place of safety for a period not exceeding 21 days. The hearing may renew the warrant for a further 21 days but thereafter the reporter must apply to the sheriff for a further warrant for 21 days, and such a warrant given by a sheriff can only be renewed once, with the effect that the total period for which a place of safety order could run would be 84 days. Before the sheriff can make such an extension to the order however he must be satisfied that the proceedings cannot be finally disposed of before the expiry of the order and that the extension is in the child's interests (subs.(8A)).

UNRULY CERTIFICATES

180. Section 70* of the Act empowers the Secretary of State by statutory instrument to prescribe regulations concerning the certifying of children as unruly. This parallels the provisions of section 69* in relation to England and Wales and reflects the concern about the growing numbers of children who are being certified unruly and committed to prison establishments. These regulations will probably not be drafted until the Pack Committee on unruly children has reported in 1976 and are likely to make it more difficult to certify a child "unruly."

GRANTS IN RESPECT OF SECURE ACCOMMODATION

181. Section 72 inserts a new section after section 59 of the 1968 Act, section 59A, which gives the Secretary of State the power to make grants to local authorities to provide secure accommodation in residential establishments either by themselves or in conjunction with another local authority or by providing a grant to a voluntary organisation for this purpose. The chronic shortage of secure places for children has meant that many children have to be remanded to prison establishments and it is hoped that this provision will go some way towards solving this problem in the long term.

REVIEWS OF CHILDREN IN CARE

182. A new section is inserted after section 20 of the 1968 Act, section 20A,* by section 80* of the 1975 Act which requires a local authority to review the case of any child in care every six months. This brings Scotland into line with England and Wales where local authorities are required by section 27 of the Children and Young Persons Act 1969 to review cases of children in care every six months. The Secretary of State is also empowered to make regulations concerning how cases should be reviewed and may if it is thought fit substitute a different period for the six months mentioned in the section.

POWER OF REPORTERS TO CONDUCT PROCEEDINGS BEFORE A SHERIFF

183. Section 82 gives the Secretary of State and the Lord Advocate powers to make regulations to enable reporters to children's hearings to conduct proceedings before the sheriff court arising from children's hearings. Power is also given to make regulations concerning the qualifications, training and experience necessary for reporters who appear before a sheriff in court. It is understood that the Secretary of State proposes to make regulations to allow reporters who have one year's experience the right to appear before the sheriff court. This provision was inserted into the Act to clarify the position of non-legally qualified reporters who appeared before the court. It had been assumed that such persons had a right of audience but in July 1975 the Court of Session decided that the 1968 Act did not confer upon such reporters a clear right of audience. This meant that only solicitors and advocates could appear before the sheriff and created many problems as the majority of reporters do not have professional legal qualifications. This provision regularises the situation which existed before July 1975 while at the same time setting standards of experience and training for reporters.

13 Registration of Births, New Provisions relating to Children who are Privately Fostered and Committees of Inquiry

Part IV of the Act which sets out further amendments contains new provisions concerning the registration of births in England and Wales, which are examined in this chapter. Part V of the Act introduces new provisions relating to children who are privately fostered which are also dealt with in this chapter as well as the new power given to the Secretary of State for Social Services to make inquiries into the exercise of the functions of local authorities and voluntary agencies in relation to children.

REGISTRATION OF BIRTHS AND ABANDONED CHILDREN

184. Section 92* of the Act amends the Births and Deaths Registration Act 1953 by making provision for the small number of children who are abandoned and whose place and date of birth is unknown. This section inserts a new section into the 1953 Act to enable the person who took charge of the child to apply for a birth certificate. The new section, section 3A*, provides that the place where the child was found shall be treated as the registration district and sub-district for the purposes of registering the place of birth and the birth date shall be that deemed to be most likely, having regard to any evidence that can be produced. A child not born in England and Wales, or who is the subject of an adoption order made in the British Isles, or who was previously registered under this Act, with one exception, cannot be registered under this new section. A person who has attained the age of 18 and whose birth records cannot be traced in any register of births

may apply for his birth to be registered under this section provided that, of course, the applicant has not been adopted.

REGISTRATION OF THE FATHER OF AN ILLEGITIMATE CHILD

185. There are two provisions relating to the registration of fathers of illegitimate children. Section 93* of the Act inserts a new paragraph, paragraph (c)*, at the end of paragraph (b) of section 10 of the Births and Deaths Registration Act 1953. This provides that the mother of a child may register the putative father as the father of the child if she can produce a certified copy of an affiliation order (*i.e.* an order made under section 4 of the Affiliation Proceedings Act 1957) which names the person as the putative father of the child. If the child has attained the age of 16 the mother must also have the child's written consent to the registration of that person as his father.

186. Section 93* also inserts a new section, section 10A* into the 1953 Act which makes provision for the reregistration of illegitimate children to show a person as their father, where previously no person had been registered as their father. This will be permitted in three cases. First, at the joint request of the mother and the person claiming to be the putative father, in which case both must sign the register in the presence of the Registrar. Secondly, at the request of the mother on production of a declaration in the prescribed form made by the mother that the person is the father of the child and a statutory declaration by the person acknowledging himself to be the father of the child. Thirdly, at the request of the mother made in writing on the production of a certified copy of an order made under section 4 of the Affiliation Proceedings Act 1957 naming the person as the putative father of the child, and if the child has attained the age of 16, the written consent of the child to the registration of the person as his father.

NEW PROVISIONS RELATING TO CHILDREN WHO ARE PRIVATELY FOSTERED

187. In recent years much concern has been expressed about the quality of care given to children who are privately fostered,

and, despite the 1958 Children Act, about the lack of control over standards in private foster homes which local authorities have. The Houghton Committee did not report on private fostering as it was outside its terms of reference, and the Bill when it was first drafted did not contain any provisions about private fostering. However the government foresaw that the Act was likely to be the last piece of legislation relating to children for some time and inserted three amendments to the Children Act 1958. These new sections give order making powers to the Secretary of State but the regulations themselves have yet to be drafted, and will not be drafted until more research has been done and consultation taken place with local authorities.

188. Section 1 of the 1958 Act which requires local authorities to satisfy themselves as to the well-being of children in their area who are privately fostered is amended by section 95* of the new Act with the effect that the requirement that an officer of the authority shall visit from "time to time" is amended to "in accordance with the regulations made under section 2A of the Act." Section 2A* is a new section set out in section 95* which gives the Secretary of State power to make regulations concerning visits to private foster homes. The regulations will be similar to the Boarding Out regulations which apply to children who are boarded out with local authority foster parents, and will set specific time limits within which visits must take place. Section 2A* also requires any foster parent who has not given notice under section 3(1) to the local authority that he has a private foster child must do so within eight weeks of the regulations coming into force.

189. Section 96* of the Act inserts a new section 3A into the 1958 Act which gives the Secretary of State powers to draft regulations requiring parents who are planning to place their children with private foster parents or whose children are already so placed to give to the local authority where the children are, or are going to be, such information as the regulations may require.

190. Section 97* inserts new subsections into section 37 of the 1958 Act which enable the Secretary of State to make regulations prohibiting the placing of advertisements by

parents who wish to have their children fostered and by persons who wish to offer children private foster care.

POWER OF THE SECRETARY OF STATE
TO HOLD INQUIRIES

191. The Maria Colwell case drew attention to the fact that the Secretary of State for Social Services had no statutory power to cause an inquiry to be held, and therefore had no power to *subpoena* witnesses, require the production of documents or take evidence on oath. The Act puts this right by section 98 in relation to England and Wales and section 99 in relation to Scotland. Section 98 enables the Secretary of State to hold an inquiry on any matter related to the exercise of the functions of the social services committee of a local authority, in so far as those functions relate to children, the functions of an adoption agency, the functions of a voluntary organisation in so far as those functions relate to voluntary homes, a home maintained by the Secretary of State for children in the care of local authorities, and the detention of a child under section 53 (detention of children at Her Majesty's pleasure and sentences of imprisonment for children) of the Children and Young Persons Act 1933. The Secretary of State has the power to order such inquiries, or part of such inquiries should be held in private, although if no direction is given then the person holding the inquiry has power to determine whether it shall be in public or private (subs.(2)). Section 99 gives the Secretary of State similar powers in relation to Scotland.

14   Conclusion

This chapter draws together some of the general themes in the Act and looks at the implications of these for social workers. The Act's wide-ranging reforms in legislation relating to children have aroused considerable controversy within the social work profession but, as yet, surprisingly little elsewhere.

192. One major area of concern is how are the resources to be found to implement the Act. Dr. David Owen was quite clear in his message to Parliament that the provisions of the Act would not be implemented without the necessary resources being made available. In the present economic climate where local authorities are under such great pressure to cut their expenditure the additional resources required to set up a comprehensive adoption service, estimated by Dr. Owen to be an extra £5 million in addition to that already spent on adoption, will have to come from the rate support grant. In making these financial calculations however the Government appears to believe that with the introduction of better procedures in fostering and adoption local authorities will be able to reduce the number of children in long term care and thereby incur a saving. This seems to disregard some of the complex factors governing the number of children coming into and being discharged from care. Some children will be adopted as a result of the provisions of the Act, but it is equally likely that their places in residential establishments would be taken by other children, perhaps those who are the subject of a care order but have been allowed "home on trial" because of the lack of suitable residential provision, or those who have been allowed to remain in a home situation which is far from satisfactory because of the lack of alternative solutions. Finding suitable adoptive homes for the emotionally or physically handicapped child is a skilled and time-consuming task and it is clear that the economic benefits of this policy

could only be reaped by local authorities in the long term, if at all.

193. The British Association of Social Workers has pointed out that there is a danger that resources to set up a comprehensive adoption service could be siphoned off from those allocated to preventive work with natural parents. Section 2* of the Act stresses that the adoption service is just one of a range of services provided for families and their children and adoption should not therefore be used as an alternative to preventive work. Nevertheless the power given to local authorities under section 1 of the Children and Young Persons Act 1963 to carry out preventive work is a permissive power and is interpreted in different ways by local authorities. Significantly, the money which a local authority is willing to allocate for use under section 1 of the 1963 Act is usually a small proportion of what it spends on residential establishments for children. The present economic situation will affect voluntary societies, some of whom are already hard hit by inflation, and many will find it impossible to provide the range of services envisaged by section 1* of the 1975 Act unless they can do this in conjunction with their local authority.

194. The Act will place additional responsibilities on social workers to prepare reports on behalf of the courts. The local authority social worker will have a duty to investigate and submit a report to the court in applications for a custodianship order, and may be ordered to prepare a report in applications to vary or revoke such orders. In certain proceedings before the court under the Children and Young Persons Act 1969 the court may order that the child should be separately represented and a guardian *ad litem* appointed and a guardian *ad litem* may also be appointed to safeguard the interests of the child in proceedings arising from section 2 of the Children Act 1948. A guardian *ad litem* will no longer be required in all adoption applications but the Act creates a new role of reporting officers which will have to be filled by social workers. These additional duties place a heavy burden on already overstretched local authority resources in terms of manpower. If resources are diverted from prevention to the setting up of a comprehensive adoption service or fulfilling extra court duties there is a danger that more tragedies could

ensue of a kind which the Act sets out to prevent.

195. The Act moves towards giving greater legal recognition to the rights of the child. It makes the welfare of the child the "first consideration" in adoption cases and in cases of children in the care of local authorities. It gives a child a right to express his views if he is old enough on decisions concerning himself in both these cases. In proceedings related to a child, the child is no longer necessarily seen as an adjunct to his parents; the court may, and in some cases shall, order separate representation for him. All these provisions are to be welcomed.

196. This increase of the rights of children does however mean a corresponding diminution of the rights of natural parents and a growth in the concept of a parent's duties. The implications of this have aroused some concern. If a child has been in care for three years or more the local authority may assume parental rights and duties in respect of him. If a child has been with foster parents for an aggregate of three years and for the three months preceding the application, foster parents may apply for a custodianship order without the consent of the natural parents. If a child is in care for any period of time the local authority may apply for an order freeing the child for adoption if there are grounds for dispensing with parental agreement to adoption under section 12(2)* of the Act. If there is an application to dispense with the consent of the parents under section 12(2)(*f*)*, the new ground that the parents have seriously ill-treated the child, the agency will have to show that rehabilitation within the family is unlikely. The chances of rehabilitation are clearly diminished if the family lives in an area where the local authority has little or no day-care provision or where the number of social workers employed is inadequate to provide the family with skilled casework help. Children come into care for a variety of reasons, but the majority of such children are from impoverished and socially isolated families. It is these families who will suffer from the effects of the Act if preventive work declines in importance. Moreover some natural parents will feel so threatened by the new powers that local authorities have that they will avoid using local authority care in times of crisis and make other, and possibly inferior arrangements for their

children's care. They may be so worried by the time limits which the Act sets that they may remove their children from care for no other reason than to prevent the local authority assuming parental rights, or a foster parent making a custodianship application.

197. These are some of the drawbacks which the various time limits set out in the Act may have for natural parents. On the other side of the coin they do stress the importance of time in a child's life and emphasise the need to make constructive plans for a child's future. As the *Children Who Wait* study by Jane Rowe and Lydia Lambert showed, too often decisions about a child's placement are delayed. Provisions in the Act will enable there to be changes in the time limits if these are thought to be necessary and this pragmatic approach may help to allay the fears of those who feel that time limits are too arbitrary a measure to use in legislation relating to children.

198. The new concept of custodianship will give foster parents and children in their long term care some legal security in their relationship. But it has disadvantages. Natural parents may find that a foster parent could gain the legal custody of a child against their wishes. Local authorities may find that foster parents who they regard as only marginally satisfactory and who need a great deal of social work help and support apply for a custodianship order in respect of a child placed in their care. If the order is granted the local authority have no automatic right to continue to supervise the home or to give the foster parents the support they feel they need. The British Association of Social Workers believes that local authorities may become reluctant to use foster homes if the social worker hopes to work towards the rehabilitation of the child with his natural parents. The relationship between natural parents and foster parents could become strained once the natural parents become aware of the increased power of the latter. Thus although the Act sets out to enhance the status of foster parents it could inhibit the use of foster care. This would be disastrous, as good foster care is for most children one of the best forms of substitute care we can offer. Custodianship may be acceptable to some relatives as an alternative to adoption. Adoption has however become the socially acceptable means of accepting a child from a previous

relationship into the new family. A custodianship order, or in the case of a child from a previous marriage, a variation of the custody order made in the divorce court may not be as acceptable to the family, particularly as it does not involve a change of name. Nevertheless custodianship may be preferable from the child's point of view as this will not mean severing his links with one half of his natural family.

199. The new procedure of freeing a child for adoption is likely to be generally approved. As an alternative to the current consent procedure in which parental rights in respect of the child remain vested in the natural parents up until the time of the hearing of the adoption application, it offers advantages both to those natural parents who have made up their mind about adoption and wish to give their consent finally and to adoptive parents who know that if the child has been freed for adoption there is no possibility of the natural parents changing their mind at the last moment and withdrawing consent just before the adoption hearing. It strengthens the powers of local authorities considerably however as they may apply to free a child for adoption who is in their care at any time if there are grounds for dispensing with parental consent to adoption.

200. Criticism has been levelled at the Act for being a sudden and emotional response to tragic cases such as those of Susan Auckland and Maria Colwell, rather than being a considered reaction based on research. It was realised however that there was no likelihood of further legislation on children for some years, and the opportunity was taken in the Act to enable the Secretary of State to draft regulations in important areas, such as private fostering and the making of unruly certificates, which could be drafted later in a more detailed and careful way than the parliamentary timetable for the Act permitted. In an attempt to introduce flexibility into the Act section 105 provides that the Secretary of State, in addition to his power to review the operation of time limits and schemes of payments for adopters, shall review the working of the provisions of the Act three years after they are brought into force, and thereafter at five yearly intervals. In this review he must prepare a report on the operations of the sections in force which is to be presented to Parliament and, if necessary, he

may institute research to aid the preparation of the report. It is hoped that this will enable the provisions of the Act to be adjusted if they prove impracticable or inoperable. Much of the controversy surrounding the Act would be dissipated if the Act were set within the context of an effective programme of prevention of family breakdown. One of the dangers inherent in the Act is that, like the Children and Young Persons Act 1969, many of its provisions could remain unimplemented through lack of resources. Legislation has a part to play in implementing social policy but unless it is coupled with adequate resources particularly in terms of manpower and training it operates in a vacuum.

INDEX

[All references are to paragraph numbers]